GOLF FREEK

Also by Steve Eubanks

GOLF TITLES

Augusta: Home of the Masters Tournament

At the Turn: How Two Electrifying Years Changed Golf Forever

Get Yourself in Golf Shape: Year-Round Drills to Build a Strong,
Flexible Swing
with Cindy Reid

Golf Over 40 for Dummies
with Kelly Blackburn

I Know Absolutely Nothing About Golf
with Whitney Crouse

Playing by the Rules
with Arnold Palmer

Arnold Palmer: Memories, Stories, and Memorabilia
from a Life On and Off the Course
with Arnold Palmer

The Pro: Lessons About Golf and Life from Claude Harmon, Sr.
with Claude "Butch" Harmon, Jr.

Out of the Rough: An Intimate Portrait of Laura Baugh
and Her Sobering Journey
with Laura Baugh

Cindy Reid's Ultimate Guide to Golf for Women
with Cindy Reid

The World of Professional Golf (1997–2004)
with Mark H. McCormack

GOLF FREEK

One man's quest to play
as many rounds of golf as possible.

FOR FREE.

STEVE EUBANKS

Crown Publishers / New York

Published in the United States by Crown Publishers, an imprint of the
Crown Publishing Group, a division of Random House, Inc., New York.

www.crownpublishing.com

Crown is a trademark and the Crown colophon is a registered trademark
of Random House, Inc.

Library of Congress Cataloging-in-Publication Data
Eubanks, Steve, 1962–
Golf freek : one man's quest to play as many rounds of golf as
possible for free / Steve Eubanks.—1st ed.
p. cm.
1. Golf—Anecdotes. 2. Golf—Economic aspects—Anecdotes.
3. Eubanks, Steve, 1962– Travel. I. Title. II. Title: Golf freek.
GV967E73 2007
796.352—dc22 2007006727
ISBN 978-0-307-33743-6

Printed in the United States of America

DESIGN BY LEONARD HENDERSON

10 9 8 7 6 5 4 3 2 1

First Edition

To Debbie, who deserves sainthood
if there is such a thing for a golfer's wife

CONTENTS

GOLF FREEK

Origins of a Freak

Debbie said: *"You want to do what?"*

This wasn't the question I wanted to hear, especially after plopping one smelly pile of an idea onto the living room rug. *"You want to do what?"* ranked up there with the blank stare and irrepressible *"Hmmmm"* as one of the bluntest hammer-blows to my egg of an idea. It was a smackdown to the creative ego; a snicker at an unveiling; idle chatter over my most soulful ballad; a groan in response to my best joke. Expounding on my genius was in order, more detail was required, clearer communication was needed. I loved the idea, but unless I was prepared to backpedal or say, "Screw it; it was just a thought," the *You want to do what?* reaction required an immediate and overwhelming response. Fortunately, the line came from my wife, who doubled as my most senior editor, the woman charged with keeping my zaniest ideas confined inside the stucco walls of our suburban home. I was sure I could make her understand.

"I want to travel the world and play golf with interesting people in interesting places, and then write about it," I said. I could tell I wasn't gaining much traction. "Look," I continued. "I got the idea from you."

"From me."

"What's the name you've been calling me for as long as we've known each other?"

She cocked her head and gave me the kind of stupefied gaze one often sees at a Jackson Pollock exhibit. Then she said: "You mean, 'golf freak'?"

I gave a well-there-you-go wave of my arms. "Golf freak! Where do you think I got the title? I'll travel the globe, making friends, being the world's greatest golf guest, and capturing the essence of the game from the ground up."

"Are you drunk?"

"I'm serious," I said. "You have no idea how many characters you meet and how many interesting stories you find through golf."

"Sounds like a boondoggle," she said. "You do understand that 'golf freak' is not a term of endearment."

I knew that, but she didn't use it entirely as a pejorative, either. A middle-aged husband and father, I always answered "writer" when confronted with the cocktail conversation staple "So, what do you do?" But that description didn't capture the core of my being quite like the depreciatory nickname bestowed upon me by my loving wife.

I missed my sister's wedding to be on a golf trip. In fact I was making a hole-in-one on a 205-yard par three while the band played "Blue Moon" at my youngest sibling's reception (everyone says it was lovely). I also hit a high draw off the first tee at 8:16 on

July 4, 1990, two hours after witnessing the birth of my son (both mother and baby were asleep, so what was I supposed to do?). There's a putting green instead of a pool table in my basement, and copies of *The Art of Golf Course Design, American Linksland, The 500 World's Greatest Golf Holes, Discovering Donald Ross,* and *The Hogan Mystique* lie stacked atop my desk. Need directions to the corner store? "You dogleg left at the next intersection, and go down a good par five until you see it on your right. It's a tap-in. You can't miss it."

It came early. At age three, I swung my first club. By the time I was twelve, I spent my summers playing a minimum of 54 holes a day, often getting in 72 between sunrise and the time it got too dark to see the ball, the hole, or my white golf shoes. Back then, a perfect day started with me standing on a dew-strewn tee waiting for the sun to pop up enough for young eyes to see an opening drive, and it ended with me rolling putts over long and fading shadows toward an ever-darkening hole. It was during the thirteenth year of my life that Dad gave me his version of "the talk," an adaptation of the birds and bees that started with a finger in my chest, and words that I have never forgotten: "Look," he said, "anybody can get laid. It takes a man to hit a one-iron." That standard of manhood has stayed with me ever since, even though I've long since retired the one-irons for longer, harder hybrids, proving once and for all that size does matter.

My obsession is mild compared to that of others I have met along the way. Take Henry Beard, an avuncular man in his sixties who founded *National Lampoon* magazine, and who plays golf a minimum of 350 days a year. (When asked what he does the other

fifteen, Henry says, "Travel to the golf course.") Or Alastair
Johnston, president of International Management Group (IMG),
a man who owns every golf book ever published, and who also
wrote such esoteric classics as *The History of Golf Before 1600 A.D.*
and *Vardon to Woods: A Pictorial History of Golfers in Advertising.* Or
the retirees in Lady Lake, Florida, who (honest to god, a true
story) were on the sixteenth tee at Harbor Hills when their playing partner fell over dead, hand firmly clinching his pull trolley.
"You know, he hasn't been the same since his wife passed on," one
of them said when I arrived on the scene. I nodded and stared
grimly at the body. After an awkward moment, the other player in
the group said, "Well, we've already hit our shots," to which I
replied, "Then I guess you guys should go ahead and play." As if
this weren't demeaning enough, the group immediately behind
the threesome-turned-twosome included three women who cried
over their poorly deceased comrade until the green cleared. Then
they played. When two groups play through a dead guy before the
ambulance arrives, you know you're dealing with true-blue golf
freaks. I like to believe I would have waited for the EMTs to pry the
trolley from my playing partner's cold hand before teeing off.

Compelling as they are, none of these stories advanced my
cause with Debbie. She has given me grief for years about the
plaques in my office listing *Golf Digest*'s 100 Best Courses in America and 100 Best Courses in the World. Like a lot of avid golfers I
put pegs in the plaques after I've played each course, but unlike
other golfers who enjoy marking courses off their lifetime bingo
card, I only add a peg to the board when I have played one of the
courses as a complimentary guest, no fees, no discounts, none of

the grimy intercourse of commerce. That's how my golf is played these days.

I don't collect golf books (although I have plenty), golf art (an oxymoron of epic proportions), or antique golf memorabilia, nor do I take pride in multiple golf memberships, even though I am a member of eighteen private golf courses. I have no delusions about playing any professional tours. I became accomplished enough to play competitive college golf, and still enjoy teeing it up in the occasional amateur event. I even give it a whirl in local U.S. Open qualifying in the hopes that I might catch lightning in a bottle one day and make it to "sectionals," where I will have the privilege of being trounced by a non-exempt tour player. I also have no goals of cutting ten shots off my score, or adding ten yards to my drives. At some point my obsession with the game took a turn. I realized that my most enjoyable—no, most *devout*—golf experiences came when the clubs' owners, managers, professional staff, or members saw fit to make my rounds complimentary, to utter the words as I checked in: "You're our guest today."

The term "golf freak" is common vernacular among the game's most prodigious addicts, the men and women who would consider it a mortal sin to drive past a public course when you've got a couple of hours to spare. These are the people who either play, practice, or think about golf every single day of the year; the ones who keep pro shop numbers programmed into their speed dials; the ones whose idea of a great holiday weekend is 18 holes on Friday, 36 on Saturday, 36 on Sunday, and 18 on Monday with dinner and drinks in between. Golf freaks don't necessarily play well; they just play often. Vacations, honeymoons, business trips, and weekend jaunts to the country are planned around making the 7:40 tee time, squeezing in a late afternoon round, or marking another top-ranked course off the list. They are like ski bums, gear heads, or speed junkies—all titles that have worked their way into the American lexicon. Golf freaks know who and what they are, and they carry the banner with pride.

They carry it in places like Poca, West Virginia, where the pavement ends a mile from the clubhouse, or Jerome, Idaho, where there is a local rule for moose tracks in the sand traps, or Fort Morgan, Alabama, where a sign on the course warns, "No Urinating on the Greens." The tapestry and mystique of the game are found at these one-tractor courses in two-traffic-light towns from Bangor to Baja, places so far removed from Tiger Woods and the Sunday telecasts that they might as well be on the third moon of Neptune. These are places where you can always find a knowing nod, a smiling face, and a heavily accented voice spilling out the most beautiful words any golf freak has ever heard: "You lookin' for a game?"

"So, you're going to travel around the world looking for golf courses in the middle of nowhere in the hopes that you'll find some interesting stories," Debbie said. Her tone shifted from incredulity to patronizing, a singsong "There, there, honey, let's think this one through together" cadence that told me I still had a good deal of selling to do.

"That's part of it," I said. "But I'm also going to play with some famous people, Arnold for example." That was Arnold Palmer, whom I know reasonably well. "And Alice Cooper. Regular folks as well."

The slight raise of an eyebrow and tilt of her pretty head told me I was making progress.

I said: "This is about social anthropology. It's like *On the Road* without the booze, hookers, guns, and poverty."

"Oh, this is a science project!" Debbie hit her forehead with the pad of her hand. "Why didn't you say so? Will scholars be comparing you to Edward O. Wilson?"

I pulled the last trump card out of my deck. "The golf will be free," I said. "That's part of the deal."

"You're pitiful," she said.

"I know."

"When do you leave?"

"Right away."

"Pack a sweater," Debbie said, turning away.

"Do you know where I put my Western Golf Association divot tool?"

"In the nightstand next to the sleeve of Pro V1s."

No one knows a golf freak better than his wife.

Part One

Preparing to Play
(or Are You Kidding? You Get Paid for This?)

_____

ONE

Sticks and Stones

(or How Technology Saved My Game)

I've never been much of a planner. Under normal circumstances I pack for two-week trips an hour before leaving, buy birthday and holiday gifts the day before the blessed event, and make dinner reservations from my car as I pull into the restaurant parking lot. Not that I have anything against planning ahead. I'm just not very good at it.

But despite my admitted planning deficiencies, I wasn't about to venture into the belly of the golf beast unprepared.

Step one was getting a new set of clubs.

"Please tell me you're kidding," Debbie said when I'd finished my "prepared adventurer" spiel.

"I have to be equipped," I said. "If I were climbing McKinley would you deny me a new set of crampons? If I were diving the Great Barrier Reef—"

"You can stop now."

"A wet suit?"

"That's enough."

"If I were trekking the Congo—"

"I have a feeling this free golf thing is going be a lot more expensive than I expected."

A quarter-century ago, purchasing golf clubs was a simple, intimate ritual. Like the best blind dates, friends matched you up with the hottest new clubs —"Harvey, you should see the heads on those Dyna-Powers! Va-va-voom, baby!" or, "Man, did you see that MacGregor Tommy Armour driver in Jimbo's bag? Made my knees weak!"

Even armed with such endorsements, initial contact with new and untested equipment remained tentative: fear of rejection high. Once a player mustered the courage to pick up a new club, the first impression was crucial to the relationship. How it looked, how it "set up," what it felt like as you waggled it in the store all were harbingers of what would either be a fruitful or tempestuous marriage. Again, like finding a suitable date, the only technical elements worth considering were how much it weighed, and how stiff you wanted it.

All irons were "blades" in those days: thin, forged instruments with long, lean furrows connecting the tiniest of heads to tapered steel shafts. The longer ones (including those now-extinct relics, the one-irons) looked like the love children of straight-edged butter knives and custom pool cues. The leading edge (that area of the club where face meets sole) was as harsh and angular as a dull ax blade, and the top line looked like the vertical sight of a rifle scope.

Woods, now called "metals" by the tradition-challenged, were teensy-weensy whittled chunks of persimmon. A serious golfer always checked the grain in a wooden club before venturing too far, cradling the head in the palm of one hand while running the pad of a thumb along the top edge. Good blocks were honey-finished to show off a tight grain that tapered to a point near the toe. After caressing the club for a few minutes, players would invariably place it on the ground near a curb or crack, any straight line, to check the bulge and roll of the face. Loft was not an issue. As Clay Long, the former chief designer for MacGregor, told me, "All our drivers had ten degrees of loft. If you couldn't hit a ten-degree driver, tough, get a two-wood."

Looks and feel mattered most. Irons had to be "square," and woods had to look solid. Other than that, a fruitful engagement consisted of caressing a club in the presence of a pro and taking a few long, slow, deliberate swings in the shop.

Alas, those clubs and the ancient sacraments that went with buying them have disappeared like last year's money. Today, just as the youthful rituals of courtship have given way to "hooking up," buying a golf club is like online dating: You fill out personal date forms, lying to both the respondents and yourself about your abilities. No more ginger touches, no more romance: Shopping for a golf club today requires charts, graphs, high-speed Internet access, and more than a tenth-grade knowledge of aerodynamics and metallurgy.

Do you need classic 17-4 stainless 1020 carbon steel grain flow forged arc technology? Or would a blended modified U-groove milled 460cc tunite alloy cradle do? What sort of gram weight, kick point, and tapering should you choose for your shafts? And what head-weight configuration produces the optimum shot pattern while reducing drag and maximizing energy transfer at the moment of inertia? Oh yeah, and what about COR, the haughty acronym for "coefficient of restitution," the percentage of energy transferred from club to ball at the moment of impact?

I had none of those answers, and understood very few of the questions. So I traveled twenty feet to my laptop. A quick browser search of "new golf clubs" yielded an astonishing 182 million hits, 170 million more than "Bush sucks," and a cool 140 million more than "Viagra online."

Hacking away at the list, I started with the clubs I knew to be "hot," not because I retain an insider's knowledge of such things, but because *Golf Digest* told me so. Once a year, the game's most prestigious magazine rates new equipment, adding a few gems to what it calls its "Hot List." One of my best friends is a fellow named John Strege, who now covers equipment for *Golf Digest,* in part because he loves it, but also because he lives in Carlsbad, California, a ten-minute car ride from the manufacturing facilities for Titleist, TaylorMade, and Callaway.

So, faced with all the choices, I called him to ask what makes a club "hot." John said, "It's completely subjective, but we (the magazine editors) look at everything. We have testers at every skill level. They hit every new club and tell us what they think. Then we bring in mechanical engineers and physicists to go through the technology and separate innovation from bull. Talk about guys who speak a different language: They might as well be speaking Farsi."

"Did you learn anything?" I asked.

"Yeah, what little I understood. Like the USGA has a limit of point-eight-three on the COR: that means a driver can only transfer eighty-three percent of its energy to the ball at impact. In one of the sessions, I found out that transferring a hundred percent is a physical impossibility. Can't be done, but if you could somehow breach the laws of physics and get to a hundred percent there would be no sound. The ball would just shoot off the club: no click, no pop, nothing; silent. Those guys explained why, but I have no idea what they said."

I put that one in my trivial-knowledge-for-cocktail-party-conversation file, thanked John for the insight, and went back to the computer to try to narrow my search. The first "hottie" to catch my eye was the TaylorMade r7 460cc Ti driver, a top pick among the *Golf Digest* editors, and, according to TaylorMade, "the most played driver on the PGA Tour."

I noticed this one first because the clubhead was the size of my foot. It was hard to miss something that big, especially after the company added a bunch of sleek high-tech writing to the heel and sole plate. The designers also plunked three large gunmetal screws in the back.

The little-r big-7 460cc Ti was a meaty, manly club, the kind of instrument that makes you feel longer and stronger the moment you hold it in your hands. It's like straddling a Heritage Softail Harley for the first time: Performance is secondary; the Alpha-dog adrenaline surge is all that matters.

The club also came from TaylorMade, a company that is one of the most important historical institutions in the history of golf, a company that forever changed the way the game is played.

It all started in the winter of 1962 when a young dark-eyed Yugoslavian named John Zebelean cupped a communist cigarette in the fingers of his weathered hand and pondered his future. John had grown right sick of dung-smelling cigs from such Soviet wonderlands at Turkmenistan and Tbilisi, along with the crappy food, dirty snow, and bleak views of industrial filth. So John and his wife, Elizabeth, packed two duffel bags and slipped through the Iron Curtain with soldiers and border guards hot on their trail.

With a lot of help, John and Elizabeth made it to Italy, and later to the rolling hills of San Francisco Bay. Unlike many of their less fortunate comrades, John had a professional advantage: He was a nuclear physicist, a trade that not only made him incredibly marketable, but was one that President Kennedy would have paid him handsomely never to practice again in his home country.

John took a well-paying job developing nukes at the Lawrence Livermore Laboratories just north of San Jose where he and Elizabeth bought a ranch-style home and a Chevy. Nine years later John had adapted well to the American dream. So, on Sunday, January 17, 1971, it was no surprise when he stretched out in front of the RCA color set with a bowl of chips and a beverage and watched the Baltimore Colts beat the Dallas Cowboys, 16 to 13, in Super Bowl V. Afterward, Zebelean followed the lead of the rest of America, which was collectively too lazy to change the channel. That made the following show, the Bing Crosby National Pro-Am at Pebble Beach, the most watched golf tournament in television history at that time.

Another beverage into the final round of the tournament, Zebelean, who had never played golf and knew as much about the game as the tournament winner, a journeyman named Tom Shaw, knew about building a nuclear bomb, had an epiphany. "I couldn't believe they were actually hitting clubs made of wood," Zebelean said.

John didn't know golf, but he knew engineering. He knew that wood absorbed kinetic energy like a sponge drew water. A metal—steel, cast iron, aluminum, or titanium—would transfer more energy from the clubhead to the ball when struck with the same velocity. In short, metal woods would go farther.

This would become a seminal moment, one of those watershed events like the morning Bill Gates said to IBM execs, "Nah, I think we'll own the software and license it to you." The significance would not be realized until years later, but that afternoon, sitting in front of the television on a lazy Sunday, John Zebelean first conceived a hollow, metal-headed golf club, a "metal wood" for lack of a better description, one that would be more forgiving, more adaptable, more durable, and easier to hit.

Metals had been tried before. The British patent office granted a patent to the Currie Metalwood in 1891, the same year Old Tom Morris drew his first routing for a new course in Gullane called Muirfield. Steel shafts made their first appearance in 1891 as well. Unfortunately, metal craftsmanship was still stuck in the steam locomotive age. The Currie Metalwood, for all its good intentions, was a thick hunk of iron on a rebar shaft, so heavy it was all but impossible to swing. After a few dislocated shoulders and blown rotator cuffs, the Currie Metalwood joined the rake-toothed wedge in golf's curiosities cabinet where it stayed until John Zebelean took another look.

Zebelean tinkered for years. His initial lack of knowledge of golf was an advantage; he approached the process from a pure engineering perspective, a first in the more-art-than-science world of club design. But knowing even less about marketing meant that his designs didn't sell very well. A few driving ranges bought the metal-headed woods as rentals—let's face it, no matter how badly you swing, it's hard to scratch a stainless steel head—but that was about it.

Enter a gregarious young club salesman named Gary Adams, the son of a club pro, and the kind of polyester-wearing backslapper who could sell anything, including Zebelean's dull gray cast metal wood, a club that looked awful and sounded worse. Adams called the new venture TaylorMade, and he beat a trail to every retail shop he could find trying to convince golfers to give Zebelean's driver a whirl.

In 1979, Adams convinced a tour pro named Jim Simon to hit the TaylorMade driver on the range at La Costa Golf and Country Club. Simon, who was hitting three-woods to his caddie standing at the 240-yard marker, looked at the club, grunted, pounded a mound of turf into a makeshift tee, threw down a ball, and hit the driver off the dirt.

The caddie's head went up and then back as he watched the ball fly thirty yards farther than any shot Simon had hit all day.

The following day, Simon put the TaylorMade metal wood into play at the Tournament of Champions, an event that would have gone largely unnoticed had Simon not been paired with Jack Nicklaus in the first round. After Simon hit his new metal contraption past Nicklaus on the first two par fives, Jack was heard grumbling that "it sounds like he's hitting a beer can."

Three months later, Simon had pros lined up on the range at Atlanta Country Club during the Atlanta Classic to hit his loud new driver. "Jeez, the whole thing's a sweet spot," one pro said. "Goddamn, that's loud," said another. Some liked it, some didn't, but everybody wanted to give it a try.

A year later, a hundred tour pros had metal woods in their bags. By 1984, TaylorMade was the number one driver on the PGA Tour. Four years later, wooden golf clubs, the handcrafted Samurai swords of the game for almost 400 years, were obsolete. And the master craftsmen who had spent a lifetime carving them joined buggy-whip makers and blacksmiths as casualties of what economists dryly call "a paradigm shift." Louisville Golf, a leading producer of persimmon heads and supplier for Wilson, Spalding, and Hogan among others, went from a hundred-person payroll to a staff of seventeen virtually overnight.

"The bottom fell out," former MacGregor chief designer Clay Long said. "We had sixty-five highly skilled craftsmen (at Mac-Gregor) making persimmon clubs, and just like that there was nothing for them to do."

Replacing these artists was a cadre of aerodynamic engineers, metallurgists, physicists, and rocket scientists. With no more Pershing II missiles to build after the end of communism, hordes of defense contractors found themselves retooling their résumés. And in a move anticipated by absolutely no one, many of them followed the example of John Zebelean and began making golf clubs.

In five years, venerable golf companies like MacGregor, Wilson, and Dunlop went from being industry dynamos to shrug-of-the-shoulders afterthoughts. In their places came start-ups like Callaway Golf, founded by a septuagenarian textile executive and winemaker; Bridgestone, a Japanese tire and rubber company; and TaylorMade.

By the turn of the millennium Callaway was pumping $40 million into research, a sum larger than former industry leader Hogan had generated in total sales just twenty years before.

Clubs weren't the only thing that changed overnight. Because metal woods imparted less spin, players started hitting harder balls. Within a few short years wound rubber balls with soft balata covers joined persimmon heads on the ash heap. With them, a player's ability to "work the ball," hitting fades and draws, hooks and slices at will, tumbled down the priority list. Golf became a high-loft, low-spin, beat-the-piss-out-of-it-on-every-swing affair. By 1997, the year the last holdouts (Justin Leonard and Davis Love) tossed their persimmon drivers in the closet, players realized that you were better off bombing drives as far as possible and having a wedge approach, even if your ball was in the rough.

Over coffee one morning, three-time Ryder Cup player Stewart Cink told me, "Before getting to New York (for the 2004 U.S. Open at Shinnecock Hills) I watched tapes of past majors at Shinnecock. In 1995, Shinnecock looked like a long, tough test. When I got there I was surprised by how short it felt. Then, I played with Vijay Singh the first two rounds, and he hit driver on almost every hole. There were some holes where I was saying, 'Wow, why is he hitting driver? This is definitely a three- or four-iron.' But even when he missed the fairways he was able to get it on the greens. From the rough Vijay shot sixty-eight with no bogeys and made it look easy, in the U.S. Open. That's when I realized that power is the name of the game today."

Not long after Stewart and I had that conversation, Tiger Woods won the PGA Championship at Medinah with an average distance per drive of 316 yards, second only to rookie J. B. Holmes, who, in a major championship, the ultimate test in golf, averaged 334 yards per tee shot. Those numbers made it official: the revolution started by John Zebelean's ugly gray metal driver was complete.

The promise that technology would help me hit it like Tiger kept me in front of my computer for several hours. But all that science sure made my head hurt.

Did you know that the little-r big-7 460cc Ti driver features "an extra-large 460cc clubhead that has the highest MOI of any TaylorMade driver"? Or that the "ultra-thin wall technology permits clubhead wall measuring to 0.6mm, which is 25% thinner than the walls of the TaylorMade r7 quad and the TaylorMade r5 dual"?

There was more. This technological miracle "contributes to high MOI for phenomenal forgiveness," and, brace yourself, the "inverted cone technology dramatically expands the portion of the clubface that delivers high COR." If that weren't enough, the "TaylorMade RE*AX shaft with Fujikura performance technology reduces ovaling in the midsection while allowing the tip to remain flexible."

As ridiculous as all this was, I didn't lose my cool until I realized that the r7 460cc Ti came with a wrench, or as the site stated, "a TLC wrench kit," that included "hard case, TLC wrench, TLC manual, TLC cartridges (available in 2g, 6g, 8g, 10g, 12g, and 14g), an r7 TP weight kit, trajectory wheel, and a TP manual."

Not only did I have to read all this gobbledygook, I was actually supposed to use a wrench to fine-tune the thing myself. No, thank you.

Maybe I'd have better luck with irons.

The Nike Slingshot looked promising. It also splashed the "Hot List" logo across the top of an ad page, along with the added boast of being an "Editor's Choice." What also caught my eye were the initials OSS that Nike had attached to this model. Apparently, Nike had "moved the center of gravity further beyond the face, resulting in Air CG+ by deepening the slingback design, widening the dual glide sole and incorporating a lighter, hotter, cryo-steel face."

My mind flashed back to my first car, a 1967 Plymouth Belvedere with an Edelbrock 600-cfm four-barrel carburetor and a lightweight 426 Hemi. As a seventeen-year-old I had no idea what any of that meant (I barely knew enough to fill it with gas and check the oil) but I knew the words exuded *cool* as they rolled off my tongue. After an hour online, it became evident that the language of today's modern golf clubs was also designed to excite and obfuscate in equal measure.

"People want all that tech jargon," John Strege said. "Remember when Callaway first got into the golf ball business? They had two balls: Rule 34 Blue, and Rule 34 Red. One was softer than the other. Those balls were failures, because they were too simple. The box was plain and the choice was easy. People didn't want that. They wanted to be dazzled by technology. Now, every panel on a box of Callaway balls is full of data. People want to feel like they're getting the best science, even if they don't understand it."

"How are you supposed to decide?" I asked.

"You've got to get fitted," he said. "You should fly out here, go through the testing centers, and get on a launch monitor. With all the technology out there today, if you don't get custom fit, you're just guessing."

"You're going to do what?" Debbie said when I told her I needed to go to California.

"I have to get fitted for clubs," I said. "It doesn't make sense to do anything else."

"Unbelievable."

"I'm sure it'll all work out."

"Oh yeah, that's what keeps running through my mind. 'Don't worry, Debbie, it's all going to work out fine.' "

"I'll be careful."

"Uhhhh." She wailed as she put her face in her hands.

"Not to be obtuse," I said, "but is that a 'yes'?"

Customizing clubs to fit an individual golfer (or as my father called it, "carving the arrow to suit the Indian") is nothing new. In fact, the oldest known set of clubs in existence, the "Troon Clubs," so-called because they were housed in the clubhouse at Royal Troon near Ayrshire, Scotland, for the better part of a century, was a custom set. Found in the boarded-up cupboard of an old farmhouse, the circa-1500 set is now on display in the World Golf Museum at St. Andrews. But back when Bill Shakespeare was a precocious tot, the Troon clubs—six woods that could be mistaken for street hockey sticks, and two irons, the heads of which look like campfire spatulas—were custom-made for some prominent Scottish citizen with the initials J.C. (we know this because those initials are stamped on the heel of the irons, and in several places on the woods).

It's doubtful that whoever made the clubs went to great lengths to "fit" J.C., although the clubmaker did know enough about the golfer's game to add a small cleat to the toe of one of the irons, thus allowing J.C. to dislodge his errant shots from gopher holes and off-the-beaten-path piles of rock.

No record exists of how many shots the custom set shaved from J.C.'s score, but throughout the subsequent 500 years, golfers like him have clung to the fanciful belief that if they could only find the right clubs—divine instruments constructed to mask their inefficiencies—all their shanks, slices, nips, yips, and flubs would vaporize.

I kept all that in mind as I pulled my rental car into the guest parking space at the Ely Callaway Performance Center, a glistening low-rise structure in the dry hills of north San Diego County. Other than the name over the door—a brand that has become ubiquitous in the game—the front of the building offered no hint that this was a golf company. It looks like any of thousands of software, microchip, biotech, or aerospace buildings in Southern California.

It doesn't resemble a manufacturing plant because, with the exception of some boutique assembly, very little clubmaking goes on there. Most of the heavy lifting takes place in Guandong, China, at a plant with a far grimmer persona than anything in the Golden State. A few people get their hands dirty in Carlsbad, assembling custom orders in front of a Plexiglas window like pizza makers at Papa John's, but the majority of the people in these buildings are designers, engineers, and marketers, a clean-fingernail, freshly-combed-hair crew for whom building a golf club consists of sitting in front of a computer screen and drawing it with a mouse.

My first stop was the indoor hitting bay where a bank of cameras that would make Heidi Klum blush was mounted at various angles to capture my every move.

"It's the same technology NASA uses to photograph Shuttle launches," Phil, my fitting specialist, said as I reached out to touch one of the cameras. This was a nice way of saying "Hands off, Klutzo," so I retreated to the center of the turf mat.

"Go ahead and hit a couple of five-irons and let's have a look," Phil said.

So I whacked a few shots all of six feet into the bulls-eye of a white mesh net. The net was there to keep shots from ricocheting around the room and crashing into the computers and cameras, which wasn't very comforting. I harkened back to the story Arnold Palmer tells about a driving net he endorsed early in his career. "We scheduled a grand launch of the Arnold Palmer Driving Net during the Mobile Open in Alabama, and a gaggle of reporters and photographers crowded around to watch me hit the first ball," Arnold said. "So, I teed up a ball and hit a solid drive straight through the back of the net. The ball flew right over Jim Ferree's head as he was lining up a putt on the eighteenth green. I'm pretty sure I said a bad word.'"

It's hard to shake a story like that when you're hitting balls beside a million dollars' worth of cameras and computers. I winced in the middle of every swing.

"Good numbers," Phil said, which was, I assumed, what club fitters said instead of "good swing."

"It felt like a toe-hook," I said, meaning that I hadn't exactly whiffed it, but the swing was anything but tour quality.

Phil smiled and shook his head. "Maybe," he said, pointing to his computer screen, "but this shows it was pretty solid."

Once upon a time, player feedback mattered. For example, years ago MacGregor engineers went down to Loxahatchee Club in Jupiter, Florida, to show Jack Nicklaus the new custom wedges they'd made for him. Jack dropped three balls in the fairway and hit a twenty-, a thirty-, and a forty-yard pitch. Then he handed the wedges back and said, "The grooves are too deep. Makes the ball go too low." The engineers didn't say "bullshit" out loud. They just hung their heads and flew back to Albany. A few days later, Clay Long poured bondo into the grooves. "Be damned if he wasn't right," Long said. "When I made the grooves shallower, the ball flew higher on short shots."

I'm no Jack Nicklaus, but I knew a toe-hook when I hit one.

"That's not what I'm seeing," Phil said. In fact, the computer he was studying showed a series of graphs that could have been mistaken for an EKG of someone in the throes of a heart attack.

"Clubhead speed, launch angle, spin ratio, and ball speed look pretty good," he said. "Why don't you hit a few more?"

So, I did, flinching with each successive swing as my mind screamed "Don't shank it off the wall!"

"Okay, that ought to do it," Phil said. "From what I've got here, I think the X-18 with an S-300 shaft is perfect for you."

"Uh-huh."

"The clubface is pretty square at impact. I see no reason to go with anything but a standard length and lie angle. We'll keep this information on file. When you're ready, just call. We have your specs in the system."

Then Phil raised the doors in the back of the testing center and revealed a backyard that made my legs tremble.

"This is our testing range," he said, waving a hand across the horizon like Ed Sullivan introducing the Beatles.

For a moment I couldn't speak. It was the most immaculate driving range I had ever seen, a garden that would have made the men at Augusta National turn the color of their tacky coats with envy.

"Oh my god," I said.

"Pretty impressive, isn't it?"

I stared for a few more seconds, drinking in every detail, and reminding myself that this was a driving range. After a minute or so I realized that some of the grass in the distance was a different hue.

"Are shadows making that grass look darker?" I asked.

"Oh no," Phil said. "We have four different types of grass out there so we can see how the ball reacts when it lands on different agronomic surfaces."

The surprises didn't end there. A row of what appeared to be red soda bottles stood like little soldiers at fifty-yard intervals down the center of the range. "Are those sprinkler heads?" I asked.

"No, those are weather sensors," Phil said. "They measure temperature, wind speed, and relative humidity at every point during the trajectory of the shot."

I put a hand on his shoulder and said, "That makes it official, Phil: Your ability to measure just exceeded my ability to execute."

Poor Phil never got the joke.

The TaylorMade fitting system was even more jaw-dropping. Indoors again (with the ubiquitous net), the expert referred to its setup as a "Mat Room," because swings weren't so much "recorded" as "matted." Not that semantics mattered: After I wriggled into a specially designed black vest, an ill-fitting glove, and the Velcrohinged straps that attached to various sensitive body parts—all necessities for accurate "matting"—I felt more like a mummy than a golfer.

"These are the same sensors Tiger Woods wears when he's making his EA Sports games. They allow the computer to track your motion."

This tidbit came from Rob Stocke, my certified instructor and fitting specialist for the day.

"I feel like Tiger," I said.

"It's not too restrictive. After a few swings you forget about the sensors."

"I don't know about this," I said.

"You'll be fine. Hit a few until you get comfortable."

I did as I was told. Five swings in, Rob said, "Let's have a look."

An animated image popped onto the screen. The details weren't complete—no hair, skin, or clothing—just a gray, wireframe outline of what was, unmistakably, my golf swing.

Not only could the computer animate my swing, it could stop, start, and view me from any angle as if the camera were flying around in space. It gave the whole thing a Carrie Anne Moss–in–*The Matrix* kind of feel.

"We can also superimpose your image over the image of a tour player to see how you stack up," Rob said. "Let's see if I can find someone in here who matches your body type."

As he scrolled through his tour database, I thought, "Maybe it'll be Tiger, or Adam Scott, or Camillo Villegas. I've been working out."

"Here we go: Let's try Darren Clarke."

"Darren Clarke! I'm not that fat!"

"Darren's lost a lot of weight recently."

Before I could launch any further objections, Rob pecked away on the keyboard until another animated image very similar to my own popped onto the screen.

"Is that him?" I asked, wondering if cigar-smoking, Guinness-drinking, potato-eating Darren Clarke and I had, indeed, become one and the same.

"Darren's a little taller, but it's close," he said.

"Ow."

Adding insult to injury, Darren Clarke's image superimposed almost perfectly over mine . . . until we began our golf swings. Then it became painfully apparent who held fourteen worldwide professional titles, and who thought any score close to par without mulligans was a Hall of Fame accomplishment.

For several minutes Rob replayed the recording back and forth, not saying much, but stopping it at various frames to highlight the stark differences between Darren and me. Finally, he said, "Have you learned anything?"

"Oh yeah," I said. "Too much truth can be a bad thing."

Demoralized and clubless, I headed home.

"How'd it go?" Debbie asked.

"Don't ask."

"So, no new clubs?"

"I guess I'm stuck with what I have."

"Is that a bad thing?"

"Not if you like driving a Model T."

I couldn't help noticing the tiny wrinkles of a smile around the corners of her mouth.

"Ann Cain called," she said.

"What did she want?"

My neighbor Ann is the Titleist rep on the LPGA tour, which means she travels twenty weeks a year keeping the best women golfers in the world in Pro V1 golf balls.

"The Titleist people are having a demo day on the range. She thought you might want to walk over and give them a try."

"Here?"

"At the range," Debbie said, pointing to the range at our club, which was no more than 300 yards from our front door.

Five minutes later, I was hitting balls at my home club with Titleist's new irons.

"How do those feel?" Ann asked.

I hit a high fading five-iron just shy of a flag I knew to be 200 yards downrange. "How do they feel?" I repeated. It was such a refreshing question that I let it linger in the air for a few seconds.

Then I cradled the clubhead in the palm of my left hand and ran the pad of my thumb along the top line from the hosel to the toe.

"Perfect," I said. "They feel perfect."

TWO

Secrets in the Dirt

(or Oh My God, Are You Double-Jointed?)

You can't strike out with a new set of clubs without getting a modicum of instruction on how to hit the things. So the next step was lessons.

Once more, I didn't have to go far to begin my journey. Half the books in my office are devoted to golf instruction, ranging from the ancient (*The Gist of Golf,* by Harry Vardon) to the modern (*How to Find Your Perfect Golf Swing,* by Rick Smith) to a combination of old and new (*Classic Instruction,* by Bobby Jones with editorial support by Ben Crenshaw), to the cerebral (*The Golfer's Guide to the Meaning of Life,* by Gary Player), to the silly (*How to Win at Golf Without Actually Playing Well,* by Jon Winokur), to the redundant (*Dave Pelz's Short Game Bible* and *Dave Pelz's Putting Bible*). There are numbers books: *Four Moves to Winning Golf, Five Fundamentals, 50 Greatest Golf Lessons of the Century,* and the *Ultimate Drill Book: Over 120 Drills Guaranteed to Improve Every Aspect of Your Game.* I have books in need of new titles, like *Better Golf,* which beats spending twenty bucks for a manual on how to play worse, and *How to Feel a Real Golf Swing,* as opposed to all those fake swings you feel now. Then there's *Gravity Golf, Holographic Golf, Practical Golf, Golf for Dummies,* and *Golf Can't Be This Simple,* the latter of which seems self-evident with all that practical, holographic gravity for dummies working against you.

I find it interesting that the two greatest players in history, Jack Nicklaus and Tiger Woods, have never relied on catchy titles. Nicklaus wrote *Golf My Way,* not to tell average players how they should play, but to explain how he did it. Tiger followed Jack's model. His book, *How I Play Golf,* doesn't have a word of "you should do this" advice in its 306 pages. All Tiger does, as the title implies, is tell you how he plays. The rest is up to you. Of course, Tiger's book could have been a lot shorter. As Stuart Appleby told me: "It's pretty simple really; you generate a hundred-twenty-five-mile-an-hour clubhead speed, hit nine-iron or wedge to every par-four, reach every par-five in two, and make every important putt: do that and you'll be just like Tiger."

Perusing my bookshelves, I also saw several volumes with my name on them, which led me to question the certitude of many of the titles. I coauthored *The Ultimate Guide to Women's Golf,* and *Get Yourself in Golf Shape.* Being neither a woman nor someone in particularly great shape, I began to wonder how much blarney passed for good golf instruction.

I also marveled at the sheer volume of "how to" tomes. My modest office housed 266 golf instruction books, but that doesn't make a dent in the total books in print. A quick Amazon search puts the number of "you can play better golf" books somewhere in the 9,000 range. That doesn't count the fifty years' worth of golf magazines, each with at least one article guaranteed to "Cure Your Slice . . . And This Time We Really Mean It!"

Golfers will do anything to find the "secret," including filling their libraries with the musings of long-dead golf pros while flying around the globe to take lessons from some famous living ones. There are even books on how to take lessons!

I've had the great fortune of meeting most of the best and worst golf instructors in the world, all of whom do yeomen's work regardless of their proficiency. I know. I used to be that guy on the range giving bad lessons to worse players.

Before embarking on a career as America's most shameless golf guest, I gave the teaching pro thing a shot for a few unsatisfying years. Only a few weeks into the job I realized how much people expect out of their pros. "Why can't I hit a draw?" "Why can't I hit it twenty yards farther?" "How do I fix that banana slice?"

Had I been honest I would have said, "You can't. And you shouldn't try. You have no talent, coordination, or athleticism. Lower your expectations and learn to play with the game you have." But students don't want to hear "You've got no chance," even if it's true. Someone with a looping swing and no leg drive should be told, "Look, you're always going to slice the ball. That's the swing you've grooved, and the one you'll always have. The only alternative is a low pull, which is worse than what you're hitting now. Just line up left, play for the slice, and learn to chip and putt like crazy.

Do that and you'll play better." Now *that* would be a lesson worthy of your time and money. But it's one you'll never get.

The final straw came on a sunny Sunday when a half-deaf octogenarian, a retired judge, came to me and said, "I can't get my two-iron high enough."

"What the hell are you doing with a two-iron?" I said, which instantly placed His Honor in the never-going-to-me-for-another-lesson category.

I couldn't have cared less. Not only did the judge border on senile, every joint below his waist was titanium. Plus, the guy couldn't hear a train whistle from twenty feet away without hearing aids nestled like bird eggs in the hair of his ears. Unless he planned on using it for a walking cane, the judge needed a two-iron like I needed a spacesuit.

After failing to convince the old bat to break the two-iron over a nearby rock, I went to the range and did my best to get him into something resembling impact position. There is only so much a man in his eighth decade of life can expect, and only so much a young instructor can do. So I helped him move his hands to waist high, and cock his wrists. I held his left arm with my right hand and grabbed the shaft of the club with my left.

"Now, do you feel that?" I asked. "That's where you should get the club right before impact."

Then I let go, and stepped back—just not quickly enough.

Before I could fully leap out of the way, His Honor threw the clubhead straight down at the ball. The result would have been a cold shank had my knee not gotten in the way.

Never having been shot with a .44 magnum, I can only throw

it out as a conceptual example of what it feels like to be clipped across the patella by an enthusiastically thrown two-iron.

I let out an almost inaudible peep as my vision blurred. Then I hopped, hobbled, doubled over, and puked.

"Yeah, I think I've got it," the judge said as he continued to practice his swing. "It's all in the hips."

For that reason alone, I carry the utmost respect for those pros who devote their lives to teaching the game. You see them on lesson tees everywhere, holding court, making swings, and imparting every morsel of knowledge they've gained in their golfing lives.

What do they get for their tireless efforts? Most golf instructors ("coach" is the moniker most prefer these days) make about $30 an hour, less than they would driving a UPS truck. The crème de la crème do a little better, making around $100 an hour. Only an elite handful make more.

But even the best haven't rid themselves of the spastics who couldn't break 100 if their children's souls depended on it. Butch Harmon, the number-one-ranked teacher in the world and someone whose stable of students reads like a Who's Who of tour players, loves showing videos of what he terms his "greatest hits," images of students in the throes of unnatural, double-jointed spells that could only be called golf swings by the most gracious or imaginative. He has cameras installed in the hitting bays of his Vegas teaching center, an enclosed building with large garage doors that open to a driving range. Golfers hit balls from mats out the doors and down the range.

Or so goes the theory. In one of his favorite clips, a pudgy

Asian man swings a three-wood with great vigor. Unfortunately, the ball scrapes across the top of the club and takes out two ceiling tiles in Butch's building. On the video, chunks of polystyrene and insulation can be seen showering down as the student hangs his head and walks away: a moment captured forever on Butch's hard drive.

"But that's not the best one," Butch says through a cacophony of laughter. A few keystrokes later a new image appears: this one of a middle-aged man with gray hair and pasty jowls. "This guy hits himself in the eye."

Sure enough, with a swing so athletically challenged one wonders if the student thought his $750 an hour would buy him a new body, the club bounced off the mat a full foot behind the ball, making contact with the Titleist at such a glancing blow that it missed the nine-foot-wide opening, hit the corner of the building, ricocheted backward, and caught the student squarely in the eye. With a dial the size of a volume control on a 1970s hi-fi, Butch runs the scene back and forth, slowing it at the moment of impact.

In the background, Butch could be seen raising his arms and ducking as the ball flew back. Then he ran over to his student.

"Butch, what did you say to the guy?" I asked.

"After I realized he wasn't hurt, I said, 'Buddy, I'm not going to charge you for this lesson, because I'm going to show that video for the rest of your life.'"

I haven't paid for a lesson in . . . come to think of it I've never paid for a golf lesson, and not because I regularly hit myself in the eye. As a budding junior golfer of some talent, I found teachers who were more than happy to offer their opinions on the game for free in the hopes that I would become something more than a kid with bad acne and a good swing. As college golfers, my teammates and I were showered with tips, techniques, and teaching philosophies, again all free. Once out of college, I was "in the business" (a phrase used exclusively by golf pros and porn stars to describe their profession) as an assistant pro, then a head pro, then an unemployed head pro, then a club manager, ditto unemployed club manager, then, mercifully, as a writer. In all those iterations I never wanted for instruction. A tip here, a lesson there: We're all in this thing together, aren't we?

The best lessons are often the shortest. Burt Seagraves, a surly old Georgia pro who once taught Larry Nelson, took one look at my swing and said, "What are you trying to do?"

"I'm trying to draw a three-iron," I said.

"Well, don't do that," Burt said, and the lesson was over.

I received similarly short, simple advice during a conversation with five-time British Open champion Peter Thomson. "You know, in my day I never carried a pin sheet," Peter said with his clipped Australian accent. "I realized that if I hit it in the middle of every green, the longest putt I was likely to have would be twenty to twenty-five feet. On six or seven holes I'd be pretty close. Any more information than that just muddles the matter."

Those are the lessons that stick in your brain.

So I was thrilled when I realized that the first instructor on my quest would be Bob Toski, the leading money winner on tour in 1954, the godfather of the modern golf school, a member of the Teachers Hall of Fame, and the most animated octogenarian this side of Bob Barker. Toski, who at 120 pounds was once a bantamweight boxer, was also the king of the one-liner.

"You have to stay loose and free to swing a golf club," Toski yelled as he bounced around like someone auditioning for the geriatric version of *Dancing with the Stars*. Then in mid-prance, he swung a five-iron and hit a flawless shot 160 yards. The dancing resumed before the ball hit the ground.

"Movement keeps you loose. Once you're still, tension sets in. Free hands and arms move the club. The body follows."

For three days I was fortunate enough to get a few hundred of those quick tips from Toski. I, along with three other golf writers, had been invited to the Sea Island Club, a 54-hole complex with a forty-room inn that is an inn in the way Biltmore House is a vacation home, to experience the three-day, four-night, all-inclusive Sea Island Golf School.

We had other instructors in the group as well. Jack Lumpkin, a former tour player who now teaches Davis Love III, was there as the anti-Toski, a soft-spoken guy who could step in before Toski spontaneously combusted. We also had Jim Ferree, a two-time winner on the regular tour, and winner of twenty-one Super Senior events on the Champions Tour. All you need to know about Jim Ferree is that he is the model for the Champions Tour logo, the silhouette of the guy in knickers finishing his swing. (Ferree is one of only two living athletes whose likeness is the model for their leagues. The other is Jerry West of the Los Angeles Lakers, whose silhouette dribbling a basketball has been the NBA logo for years. Ferree is also the guy who told a rookie named Payne Stewart that he should think about distinguishing himself on tour by wearing knickers.)

But Toski didn't give us much time to talk to the other guys. Bouncing and shuffling like a miniature Muhammad Ali, Toski shouted, "If you stay tension free and let the hands and arms lead the swing, you get . . . what?"

We looked at him blankly.

"*A golf shot!*"

We all nodded.

"And the ball goes . . . where?"

Again, no one answered, although a couple of guys raised fingers and ventured a point down the range.

"*Straight to the target!* Does anyone have any questions?"

I raised my hand and said, "Is it true you bit a guy who said he couldn't feel the club releasing?"

The story went like this: Toski was giving a lesson on the path the arms take on the downswing. When the student kept saying, "I can't feel it. I can't feel it," Toski became so frustrated that he bent down, bit the guy's arm, and said, "There, can you feel that?"

After years of hearing (and repeating) that story, I wanted to know if it was true. First, I got an earful on my improper golf phraseology.

"Release the club?" he screamed. "Release the club?"

He looked like those nitwits who walk on hot coals. Then he grabbed a club and took a vicious swing, opening his hands after impact. The club helicoptered downrange with the distinct *whop, whop, whop* of a well-thrown five-iron.

"That's releasing the club!" he shouted. "That's not a . . . what?"

"I don't . . ."

"A free-arm golf swing!"

There was a momentary pause. We were too scared to say anything lest *we* be hurled down the range. Finally, I broke the silence.

"So, did you really bite the guy?"

"It didn't break the skin."

Before the day was complete we were treated to more phraseology demonstrations. *Charlotte Observer* columnist Ron Green pushed a shot thirty yards right of his target, and Toski grabbed both his shoulders. He pulled Ron's nose to within inches of his own.

"What do you think you did there?"

"I felt like I got the club stuck behind me," Ron said, demonstrating a move we had all seen Tiger make hundreds of times after hitting a right-to-right push.

Another flea-on-a-dog's-back dance ensued with Toski screaming, "Stuck behind you! Stuuuuuck behind you!"

He grabbed Ron's club, almost pulling him to the ground. Then he took another swing, this time releasing . . . oops . . . letting go of the club halfway through the downswing. The clubhead stuck in the sod two feet behind the ball. There was a *thunk* as the head disappeared in the turf. The shaft quivered like a javelin.

"*That's* a club that's stuck behind you!"

Finally, we broke into individual sessions. Toski came over to watch me. After a couple of shots, he said, "Steve, you've got the best swing in this class."

That was like calling me the world's smartest imbecile. Anything airborne that flew past the 150-yard marker was stellar in our group.

"What do you see?" I asked after a couple more swings.

"Wow, you've got a great setup," he said, which pumped my self-worth into the stratosphere.

Then he said, "But you shut the clubface a foot into your backswing, and everything goes downhill from there."

"Oh."

"Ben Hogan told me once that nobody who plays with a closed clubface makes it," he said. "So, I said to him, 'How 'bout Ralph Guldahl? He plays with a closed clubface.' Hogan thought about that for a second, shook his head, and said, 'He'll never last.' Sure enough, he was right."

"Didn't Guldahl win three majors?" I asked.

"Back-to-back U.S. Opens and a Masters," Toski said, punching each word by hitting me in the shoulder with his right palm. "But after that his game went away and he never got it back."

"So, I swing like Ralph Guldahl?"

"Oh no, you're not that good."

After being smacked around by Toski for three days, I ventured south to Ponte Vedra Beach, Florida, for a second dose.

There is one universal rule of golf instruction: No matter how good you think you are, any instructor worth his or her salt will slap your self-esteem into the nearest water hazard. Cindy Reid, the director of instruction at TPC Sawgrass and my regular teacher, never sugarcoats her analysis. Cindy was a Junior Olympic downhill skier and a starting fast-pitch softball pitcher for Arizona State before she ever picked up a golf club, so she had little patience for prima donnas who'd played golf their whole lives.

"I can do this, and I never picked up a club until I was twenty-two years old," she would say. "What's your excuse?"

"Cindy, you struck out Barry Bonds with a softball and were a couple of seconds slower than Picabo Street in the giant slalom," I would answer. "You think natural athleticism might have something to do with it?"

"No excuses," she would answer. "That golf ball's sitting still. You can train yourself to hit it."

Cindy was already on the range when I got to Ponte Vedra. Her student was a middle-aged woman wearing an orange skirt and matching knit sweater with a green alligator eating golf balls on the front. Cindy had the woman hitting hip-high to hip-high punch shots with a wedge.

"By hitting shots like this solidly on the face, you see that you're actually hitting it farther and straighter than you were with your old, full swing," she said.

The woman appeared giddy as she hit a few more punch shots to a nearby flag. "Amazing," she said. "It's wonderful."

"Keep working at it," Cindy said.

Five minutes later she walked over to where I was warming up, and said, "Okay, let's see what you've got."

I hit a couple of seven-iron shots, and she said, "Oh my god!

Have you been splitting firewood? What happened to your swing?"

"I've been a little busy, Cindy," I said. "But I'm going on this walkabout to find the essence of golf, and . . ."

"Not with that swing you're not. I can't let you go anywhere looking like that."

"Jeez, Cindy, are you that blunt with Sophie Gustafson?" (The Swedish LPGA star is one of Cindy's students.)

"Of course not; she's good."

I pointed to her previous student, still swinging hip-high to hip-high with the same wedge. "So how do you go from being all sugar and nice with that lady to being such a hard-ass with me?"

"She pays."

"Good point."

I set up for another shot and she stuck the grip end of a five-wood under my chin. "Shut up and stand taller than this club throughout your swing. Do that, and I might let you hit the road."

I ended the lesson session in Vegas, where Butch Harmon, not someone who has ever been accused of sugarcoating his opinions, took one look at my swing, dropped his chin to his chest, groaned like a wounded animal, and then stood silently for a couple of minutes. It's not like I wasn't nervous enough hitting balls in the same bay where many of the greatest players in the world had practiced, but to add to my discomfort I had to look at pin flags from all four majors signed by Tiger. The U.S. Open flag from Pebble Beach said, "Butch, they said I could never win one of these. Thanks for everything." Flags from Adam Scott's wins were there, too, along with thank-you notes from Stewart Cink, Fred Couples, and Mark Calcavecchia.

Then there were the videos I'd seen. In addition to the "greatest hits" segments, Butch had all his good students saved on his hard drive. One clip showed Tiger hitting three-woods from the very mat where I now stood. After one swing, the world's number-one player hurled his three-wood out the door, a marvelous display of temper. Once the club hit the ground (out of the picture) hockey legend Wayne Gretzsky peeked around the corner, grinned, and said to Tiger, "Have you ever thought about taking up tennis?" to which Tiger responded, "You ever thought about screwing yourself?"

Butch also had recorded a very pale, plump, middle-aged Mark Calcavecchia hitting balls in shorts, a sight akin to seeing your mother French-kiss her cousin. Then there was Natalie Gulbis hitting drivers, which was also memorable for altogether different reasons. I saw Ben Crane wiggling and jiggling through a pre-shot routine looking like a man with Tourette's syndrome, and Catherine Zeta-Jones wiggling and jiggling just because she could.

I couldn't help wondering how long my digitized likeness would remain in the system. From the grunts and groans I was getting from Butch, I gathered the answer was not long.

After several more swings, he finally said, "Have I ever told you about the lesson my brother Dick gave?"

I'd heard hundreds of Dick Harmon stories.

"So, Dick's teaching this guy who's really having trouble," Butch said, waving his arms as he often does when he gets revved up by a story. "The guy can't hit it a lick. So Dick says, 'Okay, grip the club and set up.' The guy does. Then Dick says, 'Now, open your hands and drop the club.' The guy does that. The club falls on the ground at his feet. So, then Dick says, 'Okay, now back away very slowly, and don't pick it up again.' "

"Thanks, Butch."

"Any time."

That was where the journey ended. After being privy to some of the most valuable one-on-one instruction available in the game, I left Las Vegas knowing that I'd discovered the ultimate truth about golf. You have to find it yourself where Ben Hogan found it in the 1940s, and where Tiger Woods is finding it today. The secret to golf continues to reside where it always has: buried somewhere in the dirt.

THREE

Golf and the Mental Midget

(or Sports Psychology for Psychos)

With new clubs and a new swing, the only thing left was a mental adjustment. And since a brain transplant was out of the question (despite that recommendation from my wife and several close friends), I instead crawled onto the couch of the best sports shrink in the business.

Being old-school, I agreed with Jackie Burke, winner of the 1956 Masters and PGA Championship. When asked about the plethora of sports psychologists on the driving ranges today, Jackie said, "When we were playing, everybody had the same sports psychologist. His name was Jack Daniels." Back in the day, Hogan, Snead, Nelson, and Palmer would have stepped in front of a speeding car before going out in public with a head doctor.

Not only is the stigma gone, today every top player has a therapist, although most call them "coaches" or "mental trainers." I call them golf whisperers, swamis, or gurus, little buddies who hang out with the entourage and utter such sage nuggets as "stay in the moment," "put the bad swings behind you," and "visualize positive results." If they weren't giving "attaboys" to the world's best golfers, these "coaches" could host a good-sized Norman Vincent Peale convention. Even Deepak Chopra has gotten into the act, squeezing his theories into a golf book.

My criteria for finding the "best" sports psychologist was pretty simple: Since the entire field is relatively new, I checked into the backgrounds of the most notable practicing experts, and went with the only guy I could find who had the initials M.D. behind his name.

Psychologists rank second only to evangelical ministers among professionals who pretentiously plunk "Dr." in front of their names. Most psych doctors hold Ph.D.s, some in such farflung fields as comparative religion and P.E. Of those who do actually hold advanced degrees in psychology, most haven't seen the inside of a hospital since that college kegger got out of hand.

There is plenty of psychobabble coming from the "Doctors" hovering around the PGA Tour. Just before a playoff in the British Open, one mental coach told his player, "Just be yourself out there," to which the player responded, "Well, who else could I be?" Other gems include "Play one shot at a time," which is all-time classic nonsense (no one has been able to explain how you play two at a time) and "Be patient," another line that seems useless on a tour where it takes five hours to play eighteen holes of golf.

My cynicism didn't stop me. I hopped a plane to New York, where I was to meet and play golf with Dr. Phil Lee, M.D., a guy who not only went to Yale Medical School, but who also teaches psychiatry at Weill Medical College at Cornell University and practices performance enhancement psychology in the New York area. Phil helps lots of athletes, among them New Zealander Grant Waite, who is one of the most accurate iron players on tour. My plan was to play golf with Phil at Atlantic Golf Club in Bridgehampton on a Wednesday afternoon, the universal golf day for doctors (medical or otherwise).

"I wonder what kind of care you'd get if you had a heart attack on a Wednesday."

My friend and literary agent Mark Reiter said, "Ask Phil."

Mark, who lives in Westchester County, lets me stay at his house when I'm talking my way onto the great private courses in New York, New Jersey, and Connecticut. He is also the kind of guy Harry Vardon had in mind when he said, "A great deal of unnecessarily bad golf is played in this world. The people who go on playing it year in and year out with unquenchable hope and enthusiasm constitute the game's mainstay, for their zeal is complete, and zeal that remains unabated in the face of long-sustained adversity is the most powerful constituent in the whole fabric of a prosperous pastime."

In other words, Mark is a better agent than golfer, despite boundless enthusiasm on both fronts.

"You should go on this trip with me," I said.

Mark grunted.

"I'm serious. I need a sidekick."

"Now I'm a sidekick?"

"Well, you can't exactly carry a golf book on your own."

"You are staying in my house, you know. How's that salami, by the way?"

"Good. Just think about it. You'd get to play a lot of free golf."

"Let's play with Phil first, and take it from there."

The next morning we were to drive to eastern Long Island to play the eighty-eighth ranked course in the country, pretty stout considering there are 18,000 golf courses in the United States. Atlantic was founded as the Jewish club of Long Island in 1992. The members affectionately call it Maidstein, a witty jab at nearby Maidstone, the segregated WASP club in the "enlightened liberal" enclave of the Hamptons.

I couldn't wait to get to Atlantic so I could put another peg in my "100 Greatest" board. Unfortunately, we woke up to the kind of storm Upstate New Yorkers call a "gully washer," a torrential downpour, the sort of heavens-opening-up flood that prompts farmers to draw analogies to urinating cows and pouring water from a boot. Golf was all but impossible.

"Too bad," Mark said.

"Uggghhh."

"Are you all right? You look a little pale."

"We can't play? Have you checked the radar?"

"It's worse on Long Island."

"So, can we play?"

"In the rain?"

"I brought rain gear. You need an umbrella?"

"You are insane."

"All the more reason to play with a psychiatrist."

Ten minutes later we got a call from Phil. "I think we have to bag it," he said. "I can't see driving an hour and a half in this. The course is probably closed anyway. Sorry, maybe we can reschedule the next time you're up . . . Are you okay? Your breathing's gotten shallow."

I hung up the phone and plopped on the nearest couch, cuddling a putter as I curled into the fetal position.

"You are troubled," Mark said.

"That's why I'm writing this book. If I weren't obsessed, what would be the point?"

Three hours and one mind-numbing Ralph Fiennes DVD later I was still on the couch, a smelly lump of emasculation with an empty bag of Doritos at my feet. I didn't flinch when the phone rang, and I made no effort to eavesdrop when I heard Mark say, "He's hasn't moved" and "Got any Zoloft lying around?"

A minute later Mark handed me the phone.

"It's Phil."

"Really, I'm not that depressed," I said into the phone.

"I feel bad. Why don't we go out to my club in Scarsdale and see if we can get in a few holes. I've got a rain suit."

"I do, too!" I said as I hopped to my feet.

Mark looked at me like I'd sprouted a second head. "You're going out to play?"

"Get your rain gear. We're meeting him at Scarsdale Country Club in an hour."

"It's raining."

"What, are you salt? Get moving."

Half an hour later, as we trudged toward the bag drop at the club, a group of women came out of the clubhouse having just adjourned from a long lunch. I thought I heard one of them say, "Oh dear," as we passed.

Mark said: "I can't believe we're doing this."

"It'll be great."

"No. It'll be a lot of things, but great is not among them."

As we reached the door to the locker room, a voice from behind us said, "I've got bad news."

Dr. Phil Lee, M.D., had just come out of the pro shop. He was still in his rain pants, which I took as a good sign, but the expression on his face told me that he had sad news.

"Is it closed?" Mark said with a little too much hope in his voice.

Phil chuckled. "Nobody could believe it when I asked," he said. "The pro asked the superintendent, 'Is the course closed?' And he said, 'Yes, and who the hell is asking?'"

"Uggghhhh."

"Is he all right?" Phil asked.

"I've never seen a faster mood swing," Mark said. "When you called he went from severe depression to dressed and ready to go in under a minute."

"We have drugs for that."

"So we can't play?" I asked, contemplating the lake where the first fairway used to be.

"How 'bout I buy you lunch? You can at least look out the window at the eighteenth green."

I thanked Phil and took him up on his offer. It wasn't the same as teeing it up, but with the weather slapping us in the face it was all we were going to get.

"Let's just get this out in the open up front: Golf is not a mental game," Phil said as the seafood bisque showed up at the table.

"Chess and *Jeopardy!* are mental games. Golf has a mental component, but basically, you swing a club and hit the ball. That makes golf a physical sport, maybe not as physical as football and basketball. Somebody who has no physical skill or coordination can't concentrate his way to being a great golfer."

"So, what about guys like Bobby Jones saying the toughest distance to overcome in golf is the six inches between your ears, or some such thing," I said.

"Bobby Jones could play."

"True."

"If he couldn't get it airborne he wouldn't have said that. He also said that in an eighteen-hole round only six or seven shots went the way he anticipated. That means sixty shots per round surprised a player as great as Jones. For a lot of players today, hitting six shots the way we want would drive us nuts. Bobby Jones became the greatest amateur of all time playing that way, in part because of his talent—his surprises weren't in-the-water out-of-bounds round-killing shots—but also because he looked at his missteps as 'surprises.' He kept anxiety to a minimum, getting out of his own way."

"Easier said than done."

"Sure, but it can be done. The biggest reason we can't take our range game onto the golf course, or that we play better alone than we do in front of a gallery, is what I call 'balloon flaws.' The flaws in our golf swings, the things that keep us from being tour-caliber players, inflate like a balloon when you add anxiety. If you break your wrists during your sand shots, you might be able to get away with it in the practice area, but once you add anxiety, that flaw inflates and you spend all day thrashing around in the bunkers."

"So, do you fix the swing flaw or the anxiety?"

"Both. If you want to get the ball out of the bunker every time, you'd better work on your technique. But you can also work on minimizing anxiety. Most anxiety in golf can be controlled.

"You'll always have butterflies when you tee off in front of a crowd. Tiger Woods still does. He's just been there so many times he manages to keep it in check. If you teed off in front of thousands of people five days week, twenty-five or thirty weeks a year, your anxiety level would go down, too. It's just like holding a non-venomous snake. Intellectually, you know you're not in danger, but the anxiety chemicals in your brain cause you to have the heebie-jeebies anyway. Now, the longer you hold the snake the more accustomed you become, and before you know it, you can pick it up without thinking about it.

"You experience that same anxiety on the golf course—either a fear of slicing on the first tee, or an obsession with hitting it in the water, or an irrational belief that if you miss one three-footer, you'll miss them all. The only people who don't get those feelings have worked through their anxiety, like Tiger Woods, or are sociopaths who don't feel anxious about anything. There's no clinical data on the subject, but I'd guess sociopaths make decent golfers."

"Sweating over a three-footer is a natural biological response?"

"Absolutely," Phil said. "All threats, real or imagined, trigger the release of chemicals: adrenaline, serotonin, dopamine, endorphins, that sort of thing. They change your heart rate, lung efficiency, muscle tension. The purpose is to eliminate the threat so you can return to a state of normalcy. That's why you can't wait to hit that opening tee shot. You need to get it over with so you can get off the tee and out of the spotlight as quickly as possible. Your instincts are telling you that there's something abnormal—like holding a harmless snake—and you need to either fight or flee."

"If everybody has it, how do you eliminate it?" I asked.

"You don't, but there are lots of techniques for learning to control it. In psychiatry we've discovered something called the 'magic hour' when dealing with anxiety. If you have a fear of snakes, when you confront that fear for an hour, the spigot of chemicals runs dry. You're petrified the first few seconds you're holding the snake, but an hour later, you're yawning and tickling the thing. The anxiety's gone because the chemicals causing it are gone.

"Unfortunately, the first tee anxiety comes and goes in a few seconds. You can't stand there for an hour before hitting. But you can simulate the anxiety you feel on the first tee or over a three-footer. Get a digital recorder and record all the bad things you say to yourself in your mind—"You're going to hit it fat!" "Kill it!" "You're going to miss!" "Don't shank!" Then put those on your iPod and play them over and over to yourself while you practice. After a while, you learn to tune them out."

"Can't wait to share that one with my wife."

"That's only one behavioral technique. The one that's most useful in the short-term is a form of semi-self-hypnosis. When you're approaching a pressure situation—a tee shot in front of a crowd, or a must-make putt to win a match—tense every muscle in your body, starting at your lower extremities and working your way up until you've clinched your jaw and tightened your neck muscles. Then reverse the process, relaxing each muscle group until you're almost completely limp. As you relax, draw a picture of a meter in your mind with the number ten at full tension. Then as you relax, imagine the meter ticking down to a one or two. When you get over your shot, keep your meter in mind and never let it get above a three.

"Pros have done this for years without realizing the medical applications. Byron Nelson used to say that any time he felt a little pressure, he imagined a metronome slowing down. If he forced himself to walk and breathe at the pace of the slowing metronome, he had a good chance of making the shot. Sam Snead used to say that he thought about his muscles being 'oily' when he needed to hit a good shot.

"Those are some behavioral defenses, but there are plenty of cognitive defenses, too. Getting a player to understand the consequences of hitting a bad shot is one."

"Like what?" I asked.

"If you miss a putt, what are the consequences, really? If you're playing in the final round of qualifying school and you need the putt to earn your tour card, missing it means you don't get the job you want. You don't get eaten by a tiger; you don't go to jail; you don't lose your family. And that's as pressure-packed as it gets in golf. So, the anxiety we create on the course comes from perceived consequences, not real ones.

"Sure, if you hit it in the water, you'll probably make double bogey, but so what? Tiger makes doubles, just not as many as you or me. He hits it in the water, three-putts, all the things high-handicap golfers fear. Do you think Tiger lets those shots, or the fear of hitting them, ruin his game? He gets angry, but he doesn't let fear of hitting the same bad shot again paralyze him or spoil his mood. He doesn't dwell on it."

"And most people do?" I asked.

"A lot of people dwell on a particular shot for an entire round. I worked with a woman who always hit the ball in the water off the tee on the fourteenth hole, even though the water only extended about seventy-five yards. She was a pretty good player, and the shot wasn't that difficult. She'd hit hundreds of tee shots on the range that would have easily carried the hazard, but the prospect of that hole drove her dread level out of sight.

"I asked her to take a pencil and piece of paper out on the course and write down her thoughts just before and just after the shot. No surprise, she was thinking, 'It's going in the water!' I had her analyze how often, in realistic terms, she could hit a seventy-five-yard shot. She figured she could pull it off nine times out of ten. So I said to her, 'Your anxiety level is off the charts for a shot that has only a ten percent chance of failure.' A light went on in her head. Once she realized the disparity between her anxiety and the likelihood of failure, she didn't have any problems on that hole.

"Even good players let dread affect their games. Remember when Sergio Garcia went though his spell of re-gripping the club fifteen or twenty times before each shot?"

During the final round of the 2002 U.S. Open at Bethpage, the New York crowd started counting as Sergio went into his re-grip ritual. The young Spaniard answered by giving them the finger.

"That's no different from when someone who turns off the oven by rote walks out one morning and says, 'Gosh, did I turn it off this morning?' He gets out of his car and goes back in to check, even though he turns it off every morning and there's no logical reason to believe this morning was any different. As long as that's a one-time thing, it's no big deal. But when you turn off the oven, walk out, convince yourself you didn't, walk back in, check it, walk back out, convince yourself again that you didn't, walk back in, and repeat that process dozens of times, you're in obsessive-compulsive mode.

"Ian Baker-Finch hits the ball beautifully on the range and at home when he's playing with friends. But the second he pegs it up in competition he gets the driver yips. Before he went to the long putter, Scott McCarron couldn't pull the trigger on a two-foot putt. In baseball, Steve Sax, the Dodgers' and Yankees' second baseman, was Rookie of the Year and a five-time All-Star. Then, out of nowhere, he couldn't make a throw to first, a throw he'd made without thinking about since he was ten years old. His throws became so bad that fans sitting in the right field seats started showing up wearing catcher's equipment. The same thing happened to Chuck Knoblauch. When he moved to the Yankees, his throws got so bad that he hit Keith Olbermann's mother in the head. Mickey Sasser, the catcher for the Mets, got the yips throwing the ball back to the pitcher. Mark Wohlers couldn't find the plate after being a reliable closer."

"So, how much therapy would someone who hits Keith Olbermann in the head need?"

"It was Olbermann's mom. But I have a four-visit rule. If I can't make you better in four visits, you need to go somewhere else."

"That won't do you much good on tour," I said. "You're supposed to be on the range at every major whispering 'Be the ball' in your players' ears."

" 'Be the ball'?"

"Forget it."

"I don't go to the majors. I've got a practice to run."

"Doesn't do much for your Q score as a sports psychologist."

"That's because I'm a psychiatrist."

"Good point."

Mark jumped in and said, "Phil, what kind of therapy do you recommend for a guy who gets so depressed by a washout that he can't get off the couch, and then has a complete transformation when he thinks he might get to play in the rain?"

"I don't know," Phil said, "but it might take more than four visits."

Part Two

A Good Walk Sponged

(or Golf That's Worth Exactly What You Pay for It)

FOUR

Trekking the Trail

(or You Want Gravy on Them Eggs?)

Talking Mark Reiter, friend and literary agent extraordinaire, into hitting the road with me was not that hard. He's weak and prone to peer pressure, especially if there's free golf involved.

"Where do we start?" he asked, as if this were an Everest ascent with a standard base camp.

"Alabama," I said.

"Alabama? I thought we were going to Southeast Asia. Wasn't there a China trip coming up?"

"Biggest typhoons in fifty years. The hotel we were booked into is under water."

"I didn't see anything about that."

"A billion Chinese didn't see anything about your last nor'easter, either."

"So our fallback is Alabama?"

"An investigative exposé on the Robert Trent Jones Golf Trail, four hundred thirty-two holes, ten sites stretching from Mobile to

Muscle Shoals. It's the largest golf project in the world, multiple courses scattered hither and yon. Each site's got at least twenty-seven holes; most have thirty-six or fifty-four. You can't drive two hours in any direction without hitting one. They've even got directional signs on the interstates pointing you to the first tee. All funded by the state teachers' pension fund."

"And we're going because . . ."

"They built them to lure people to Alabama. The logic was if you could get folks on their way to Florida to veer west and spend a week playing golf, you'd bring tourism dollars to the state."

"And . . ."

"We need to see if it worked. Other states are trying the same thing—Tennessee, Idaho, there's even a Lewis and Clark Golf Trail in South Dakota. So far nobody's pulled it off like Alabama. Our job is to figure out why."

"You actually sold them on this, didn't you?"

"Marketing people will buy anything. My dad's joining us for a couple of days, too."

"Your father's in on this?"

"Where do you think I inherited the gift?"

"So, back to my original question: Where do we start?"

"Glencoe, Alabama, about halfway between Rainbow City and Talladega."

"Nowhere a New York Jew would stand out or anything."

"Wear your NASCAR cap."

Golf Digest calls it one of the fifty best golf destinations in the world, a claim bolstered by the fact that for ten years the PGA Tour held its Nationwide Tour Championship at various courses along the Trail. The Champions Tour also holds its annual Alabama event at the Trail's Birmingham course. Not to be outdone, the LPGA Tour has chosen the Trail's Mobile course (Magnolia Grove) as the permanent home for its Tournament of Champions.

I had a superficial knowledge of the Trail: not much more than anyone else who reads the travel sections of magazines. I knew that a transplanted Minnesotan named David Bronner came up with the idea. As administrator of the Alabama teachers' pension fund, Bronner thought parking some retirement money in revenue-generating real estate (golf courses) to attract tourism would be a win-win. The portfolio would have a long-term real estate component, and Alabama would have something other than Space Camp and the Hank Williams Museum to attract visitors.

Once he sold the necessary elected officials on the idea, Bronner sat down with a local golf course developer and stuck pushpins in a map. They decided they wanted all the courses to be close enough that you could play one, get in the car, drive to the next, spend the night close to the first tee, and repeat the process the following day—an honest to goodness "golf trail."

Bronner stuck a dozen pins in his map. Then he made the decision to build all of them as soon as he could. He also wanted one architect to design the whole shebang. This would create consistency and familiarity along the Trail, sort of a golfer's Disney World, a place where you knew what kind of course you were going to get and what the burgers in the grill tasted like before you ever arrived.

I spoke with David Bronner about his decision to go with Robert Trent Jones, an aging Scottish golf course architect who had been a favorite of Bobby Jones (no relation) when Jones (the player) needed someone to freshen up Augusta National. Jones (the architect) was the guy responsible for the current sixteenth green at Augusta, where Tiger hit his now famous chip shot in 2005, the one where the ball slid up the hill, rolled back, and stopped on the lip of the cup just long enough for Verne Lundquist to say, "Oh . . . my . . . goodness." Jones also moved the tenth green to its current location, and built the small pond on eleven.

In later years, after Jones (the player) passed away and Jones (the architect) lost his faculties, Trent, as he was called, became the object of a running bet during Masters week. Every morning, Trent would hobble out to the second-floor clubhouse veranda and park himself in a rocking chair. Patrons standing under the big oak adjacent to the first tee would place bets on when he would fall asleep. In the last years of his life, Jones rarely made it past noon.

"I wrote letters to seven of the top architects and told them what we had in mind," Bronner told me after we swapped Jones stories. "One famous architect who shall remain nameless wrote back and said, 'I know you say you want to do fifty-four holes at your first site, but you really mean you want to do eighteen now and another thirty-six in ten years.' Another guy (whom I have subsequently learned was Jack Nicklaus) wrote back and said, 'You're a public institution, so you really can't afford my brand.' We really thought that was funny. Trent was the only designer to pick up the phone and say, 'Are you serious?' I told him that not only were we serious, it looked like we were going to have seven or eight sites locked up before we ever broke ground. I told him, 'This is an opportunity for you to create your masterpiece.'"

Mark and I made our first stop on the masterpiece list: a 27-hole club with a nine-hole par three (or "short course" in the vernacular of the Trail) called Silver Lakes, a beautiful facility in the pine-tree-laden east middle of nowhere. After making a left at a tractor dealership mere moments before the pavement ended, we stumbled upon the golf course after convincing ourselves that it couldn't be way out here.

In the clubhouse, a cheery assistant pro gave us a complimentary "marketing" receipt for our golf. Then he said, "Gentlemen, you're playing Heartbreaker to Backbreaker today."

"Playing what?" I asked.

"We have three regulation nines: Mindbreaker, Backbreaker, and Heartbreaker. You're starting on Heartbreaker and turning to Backbreaker."

"What, no Ballbreaker?" Mark said.

An evil grin crept onto the guy's face. "Wait till you get out there," he said.

My father met us on the driving range, where he was already in a foul mood. At sixty-seven, my dad, Frank, finally looked his age. A former small-college baseball and basketball player, Dad had been totally gray and twenty pounds overweight since age thirty-five, the year my youngest sibling was born and a candy striper mistook

Frank for a waiting grandfather. That would have been a great excuse for a thirty-year disposition that ranged from "blunt" to "hard" to downright "mean." But I knew better. Dad had been a crank as long as I could remember; hair had nothing to do with it.

He was hitting balls on the end of the range when we got there, still swinging good for a sixty-seven-year-old. But some things about him were stuck in a past generation.

"I hope we go out ahead of them," Dad said, waving his driver at seven women in front of him on the range. "We'll be here forever if we don't."

"Dad, they're right there," I said. "They can hear you."

"Hi, I'm Frank Eubanks," he said, introducing himself to Mark.

"Not a fan of women on the golf course, huh?" Mark asked.

"I don't mind as long as they play at night," Dad said. "You could give them miner's hats. They can't hit it out of the beam of light anyway."

"They're still right there," I said, pointing to the two groups of well-dressed women pretending to ignore him.

Mark looked at me with a "now what do I say?" expression on his face. I shrugged. Dad had what I termed "chickdar," an uncanny ability to detect any woman on the golf course no matter how far away. An LPGA superstar could be three under par and three holes ahead, and Dad would point to her and yell, "There's the holdup."

Years before, I'd seen Dad lie down in the middle of a fairway while waiting on a group of women to clear the green. When we got closer, one of the women was waiting for us, hands on her hips. "You don't think we should be out here, do you?" she asked rhetorically.

Dad replied, "No, ma'am. I think you ought to be home canning peaches."

It took Mark and me three holes to realize what the evil grin on the assistant pro's face was all about. Silver Lakes was a masochist's dream: a course so hard that I barely broke 90, and Mark and Dad were close to triple digits.

"Think they're all this hard?" Mark asked as we headed north toward Huntsville.

"If they are, this is going to be a long couple of weeks."

"Wonder if those women enjoyed it," he mused.

"They had to enjoy the course more than Dad enjoyed playing behind them."

"What's up with that?"

"It's been a hang-up for as long as I can remember. One time my mother started talking about taking golf lessons. The next week she's got new earrings and a pearl necklace."

"Did she take lessons?"

"She never mentioned playing golf again."

The next morning, after receiving the standard "You're complimentary marketing guests today . . . let us know if you need anything" greeting, we walked through the bag drop in Hampton Cove, the 54-hole Huntsville facility, in time to see the seven ladies from the day before unloading their clubs. It was only fitting that they would shadow us the entire trip, traveling the Trail like scouts, two groups of Calamity Janes in matching Dodge minivans.

"Look, Dad, your pals followed us. Must have been your charm and charisma."

"Let's hurry."

This time we did, indeed, make it out ahead of the women, not that it mattered. None of the foursomes of men in front of us set any land speed records. When we got to the fourteenth tee a twosome of women (not a part of the group of seven) caught up to us, and Dad, doing his best to make amends for his boorish behavior the day before, said, "Ladies, I want to applaud you. You play really fast for women."

"Oh my god," I said as I hid behind a cart.

"I'm trying to be nice."

"Yeah, I'm sure they took it that way."

Mark patted Dad on the back and said, "At least your heart was in the right place."

We played thirty-five holes in Huntsville. It would have been thirty-six, but on the final tee box the GPS, that nifty marvel that gives you yardage, maps, and tips on how to play the holes, flashed the dire message: "Return to Clubhouse Immediately! It's Dark!"

It didn't say "you morons," only because it didn't have to.

Giving Frank grief for his women-on-the-golf-course fetish became one of the themes of the trip, a running joke every time we saw a female who wasn't piloting a beverage cart. That said, this was the same man who had grabbed me by the collar when he caught me bragging about winning my first junior tournament at age twelve, and told me, "You keep your mouth shut when you win, and compliment your opponents when you lose," then pointed a thumb over his shoulder and grumbled, "That scoreboard's loud enough. You don't need to add anything."

Being at that age when I knew everything and Dad was the dumbest rube who ever walked, I said, "It's not bragging if you can do it."

I thought Frank was going to take my head off. He pulled the collar of my shirt until my face was within an inch of his. "Today you're a winner," he said, as if that were an insult. "Tomorrow you'll be a loser. The next day, you might be a winner again. But if you're an asshole, that's a tag you carry to your grave."

I never boasted about another victory.

I also never took my opportunities in the game for granted. The summer before I turned fourteen, I thought I had become good enough that I no longer needed to toil away on the range as I had in previous years. So Dad took me out to the course one day, but instead of dropping me off to practice, he said, "The superintendent just hired you for the maintenance staff."

I said, "I didn't know I'd applied."

"I took care of that for you."

For the next eight weeks, I stood in black knee-high water with a chainsaw in my hands. I was clearing out a twenty-acre swamp the locals called a "slue," a mineral-enriched wetland that would probably be protected by environmentalists today. In the seventies, a "slue" was the perfect spot for one of Dad's object lessons. The message was clear: I could either spend sunlight hours working on my short game, or I could put on waders and dodge snakes while clearing spindly oaks and poplars out of a stagnant organic stew.

I shared those stories with Mark as we left Huntsville and fell into what would become our ritual. Mark and I would follow Frank to our next destination on the Trail, where we would all check into a Marriott, find the nearest Longhorn Steakhouse, get a protein infusion, and fall asleep by ten. The next morning we would carbload in the hotel, play golf all day, and then repeat the process. It was the perfect guy trip.

Our third city was Muscle Shoals, home of the famed Muscle Shoals Sound Studios where Mick and the gang recorded *Sticky Fingers,* Otis Redding sat on the dock of the bay, and Duane Allman jammed with Wilson Pickett.

"This place used to be hot," Mark said. "They had a group of studio musicians everybody wanted to work with."

"The Swampers," I offered, to show that I wasn't a complete novice. "The guy who played bass for them was named David Hood. His son Patterson Hood fronts the Drive-By Truckers."

"The drive what?" Frank said.

"Nobody you'd know," I said.

"Hey, I know Jerry Reed," Dad said, pointing to an album cover on the wall of the Marriott bar. "He was the truck driver in *Smokey and the Bandit.*"

"Hey, anybody know why they misspelled the name of this town?" Mark said to change the subject.

"What do you mean?"

"Well, if it's a shoals you'd figure it would be mussel—s-s-e-l, not m-u-s-c-l-e."

I said, "You should see how they spell Phenix City."

"When I was stationed at Fort Benning I drove to Phenix City and listened to a speech by George Wallace," Frank said.

Mark and I looked at him like he'd just admitted to gassing the Kurds.

"What? He was dynamic on the stump. Plus," he pointed a finger at me, "you were twelve months old and had cried for eleven. I'd listen to Wallace all day to get away from that."

The two Trail courses in Muscle Shoals on the shores of the Tennessee River are called the "Schoolmaster" after Woodrow Wilson, the father of the Tennessee Valley Authority, and "Fighting Joe," named for Joe Wheeler, the only general to serve in both the Confederate and United States Armies. We played "Fighting Joe," a course that opened in 2004, which I found quite nifty, since Robert Trent Jones died in the summer of 2000. David Bronner assured me that the layouts had been done many years before.

No matter, the place might as well have been called "The Hundred Years War." When we arrived on the first tee, after—I'm beginning to be embarrassed to say—our obligatory "You're our guest today" greeting, the starter handed us scorecards and checked us off his list. I looked at the card and said, "Excuse me, is this a typo, or is this golf course eight thousand two hundred yards long?"

I was informed that there were no typos. From the back tees, Fighting Joe is the third longest golf course in the world.

"You don't have to play it from back there," Frank said.

"Sure I do! How many times do you get to play an eighty-two-hundred-yard golf course? I've lived this long and haven't done it yet."

"I haven't bungee jumped," Frank said. "Doesn't mean I plan to start."

Mark and Dad rode in the same cart and played a set of tees two thousand yards ahead of where I shot a tortured 87. During the round I overheard Dad tell Mark the story of how he started playing golf in the Army. "I was always a baseball player, but a buddy in my artillery unit took me out to the base course," he said. "Now, I wish I'd grown up playing golf exclusively."

This was a point Frank hammered home to me throughout my formative years. He came to every basketball and football game I played growing up, but he never let me take those sports too seriously. "Enjoy it while you can," he'd say. "Not a lot of calls for five-ten, slow, white power forwards."

During the Wednesday pro-am at a local tour event in the late seventies, Dad took me out to the range to watch one of the sweetest-swinging tour pros I've ever seen. Unfortunately, the pro was hitting balls next to a lumbering cripple of a man who could have used his clubs more effectively as crutches. "You see those two fellows?" Frank said to me.

I nodded.

"The one with the good golf swing is Don January. He's fifty years old, and has as good a chance as anybody to win this tournament. The other guy is Tommy Nobis, All-Pro NFL linebacker. He's thirty-six and will be lucky to walk from here to the first tee."

Dad didn't say, "Which one would you rather be?" He didn't have to.

And so it went: We traveled from Muscle Shoals to Birmingham; Birmingham to Prattville; Prattville to Greenville; Greenville to Dothan; Dothan to Opelika—eat, play, drive, eat, sleep, and repeat.

My father, who initially planned to stay a couple of days, never left. "I'll go home when I get tired," he said. "That's one of the advantages of getting my age: You play when you can, and stop when you want."

"Or when there are too many women on the course," I said.

By this time I had identified our constant female shadows. They called themselves the Chicago 7, league players from Cook County who traveled to Alabama every year to play the Trail. They had become so famous in Alabama golf circles that by the time my father insulted them, they were regulars in the pro-am at the LPGA Tournament of Champions, a group that got special recognition by the tour's commissioner every year.

"Would you bring your wife down here to play golf?" Dad asked Mark.

"Sure," he said. "I'm probably going to bring her down here this winter. The weather's perfect, the golf's great, the hotels are close, and the people are nice. Hard to beat that combination."

"I agree except for the wife part," Dad said. "My idea of a great golf trip is one where she doesn't have to go."

"That's my mother you're talking about," I said.

"And we've had a successful fifty-year relationship because she doesn't play golf."

"That's your secret to a successful marriage?" Mark asked.

He shrugged. "It's worked so far."

By day nine, on the road between Dothan and Opelika, Mark and I had become so conversationally exhausted that we digressed to counting Waffle Houses and reading the legend boards outside Baptist churches. In Eufaula, Mark spotted one sign board that said, "Stop Drop and Roll Won't Work in Hell."

"I have no idea what that means," Mark said.

"Don't worry: I don't think you're their target market."

"I don't know," he said. "My house mother at the orphanage made it her mission to 'save' me by dragging me to revival services."

I knew that Mark had grown up in the Hershey School, a boy's orphanage and working farm in Pennsylvania founded by chocolate magnate Milton Hershey and his wife, Catherine. The few times I had broached the subject, Mark had been straightforward if not somewhat joking about the whole situation. "Imagine my surprise when my mother told me I was moving to an orphanage," he said. "Not only that, I was going to Hershey, Pennsylvania, which would have been great except I'm allergic to chocolate."

With another hundred miles of cow pastures and Waffle Houses ahead of us, I figured now was as good a time as any to ask a few more questions. "So, how exactly did you end up at the Hershey School?"

"My parents moved to Israel from Germany," he said "My father, a soldier, was wounded by a land mine in 1949. He lived for four more years, during which time I was born. When he died, my mother moved my brother and me to Philadelphia. She couldn't speak English, didn't have a job, and couldn't raise us, so she put my brother in the Hershey School first. When I was old enough, I followed him."

"I didn't realize you were born in Israel."

"Well, we moved when I was one. It's not like I remember much."

"Mark doesn't sound like a typical Israeli name."

"My name was Meier," he said. "I remember sitting in the backseat of a car in Philadelphia, and my mother's sister was telling her that an American boy couldn't grow up being called Meier. It sounded too Jewish, I guess. So they batted around a couple of ideas and settled on Mark. I was renamed right there on the Pennsylvania Turnpike."

"Wow," I said, thinking of nothing else that quite did the story justice.

"Yeah, well, what are you gonna do?"

"So, how long did you stay in Hershey?"

"Throughout high school. I milked cows every morning and worked on the farm. We had ten boys per house with one set of house parents and their families. My house parents were Mr. and Mrs. Peterman. Mrs. Peterman was the one who made it her mission to convert the poor little Jew kid to Christianity."

"How'd that work out?"

"Not well, although one revival guy almost had me. He kept talking about being 'saved.' I was living in an orphanage, so that sounded pretty good. I went up the aisle and started talking to him, and he said, 'You need to come downstairs with me.'"

"Uh-oh."

"Yeah. So, I follow this guy downstairs into the bowels of

Baptist-land, and he put his hands on my shoulders and said, 'Mark, are you ready to let Christ into your heart?' I said, 'Sure.' So he said, 'Are you ready to love Him?' And I said, 'Yeah.' Then he said, 'Are you ready to die for him?' And that's when I said, 'Whoa, whoa, wait a minute, I thought this was about getting saved.' I was young, but saved and dying didn't seem to go together."

"Did he try to bugger you?"

"No. About the time I balked at the dying thing, I heard footfalls pounding down the stairs. It was Mrs. Peterman, who'd been looking all over the place for me. Nobody from the orphanage knew she'd taken me to this thing. Then she lost me when I headed downstairs to get 'saved.' She lit into that preacher. It was ugly."

"What happened?"

"Nothing. But on the way home she said, 'Mark, you can't tell anybody about this. Not even any of the other boys. It'll be our secret, just you and me.' For me that was better than being saved. Mrs. Peterman had breasts."

The next morning we met Frank at the Grand National golf club in Opelika, the most popular thirty-six-hole complex on the Trail. The courses in Opelika were the best of the bunch by a mile.

I found it hard to focus on the golf courses that morning. Not only were ten consecutive days of golf coupled with twenty cumulative hours behind the wheel of a car a bit excessive, I couldn't get my mind off the stories Mark had told on the road the night before. And I couldn't help wondering what I might have turned out like if the roles had been reversed. What would we have been like if he had grown up listening to Frank's hard-ass life lessons on the golf course while I had been milking cows in an orphanage? Something told me that Mark would have managed a lot better than I.

Later that morning, as Mark went to the chipping green to work on a few pre-round sand shots and Frank and I were left to roll five-foot putts together on the putting green, I took a couple of seconds to stare at my father. He still could have stood to lose about ten pounds, but all in all he was in darn good shape for a guy on the downside of his sixty-seventh year. He'd gone to a belly putter four years before, and his short game had improved dramatically. As he rolled his second consecutive right-to-left breaker in the hole I said, "Good putt. You're rolling it good this morning."

"I love the speed of these greens," he said.

After another throat-clearing pause while I looked across the range at Mark, who was losing his ongoing battle with the bunkers, I said, "You know, Dad, I'm really glad you were able to come with us on this trip."

He nodded and said, "Yeah, it's been a lot of fun." And then, "Thanks for inviting me."

With that we headed to the tee. It wasn't much, but it was as close to "I love you" as a couple of golf freaks were ever going to get.

FIVE

Golf and the Girls of China

(or "She say, 'It in the hole.'")

My trip to Asia with Mark got typhooned out, but that didn't stop me from eventually going to China. What I never imagined was how that trip would slap me in the face like a summer-storm wind.

In my thirty-plus years of playing golf, I've been fortunate enough to test my game on the finest and most prestigious courses ever built. My hand shook the first time I plugged a tee in the turf at Augusta National, and I had to take two or three deep breaths as I stepped onto the Old Course at St. Andrews. I uttered the obligatory wows when I played seven and eight at Pebble Beach, and called friends over to see whales spawn below the cliffs beside the eleventh green at the Old Head in Kinsale, Ireland. But nothing could prepare me for the jolt I would experience during my golf freak trip to the other side of the world.

My trip was sponsored by a San Francisco-based travel company (the only way to go overseas, since airlines, hotels, restaurants, and ground operators pull out all the stops for travel execs). This particular company had discovered, quite by accident, a burgeoning golf vacation market for China when, without any plan or forethought, several business clients asked if they could take their clubs to Shanghai. When the travel agents started checking out the courses they realized that the world's fastest growing economy was quickly becoming a hotbed of golf development.

My job was to give the company an expert's perspective on what a traveling golfer wants out of a trip. Pretty good work if you can get it, but even I was stunned by what I found. Not only was the golf in China better than I expected, but the accommodations and service levels rivaled anything in the U.S., and put the grim and rugged inns of Europe to shame.

But that wasn't the biggest surprise. The life-altering experience for me began as I stood outside the caddie pen at the Spring City Resort in Kunming, a "small" city of six million in south-central China, nestled in the foothills of the Himalayas just north of Laos. Kunming actually means "Spring City," so called because the town sits five thousand feet above sea level (Denver altitude) but lies close enough to the equator that every day feels like spring. Summer temperatures rarely climb above 75, and winter nights seldom dip below 50: perfect golf weather. I didn't need a sweater as I stood in front of the Spring City clubhouse, a few minutes away from my tee time at the Jack Nicklaus–designed Mountain Course, one of a half-dozen new courses popping up in the area.

I was staring out toward the big lake separating Kunming and Jinning when the club's general manager, John Lau, snuck up behind me and introduced himself. We shook hands and chatted for a second before John said, "So, is this your first trip to China?"

"No," I said, "my daughter is from here."

John cocked his head and gave me the usual "I don't get it" stare. So I whipped out my wallet and produced a recent photo of my then four-year-old daughter, Liza, who spent the first sixteen months of her life right here in the Kunming orphanage.

John's eyes widened. "Your daughter is from China?" he asked. This must have come as something of a shock since I am a blue-eyed American with melting-pot roots from England, Ireland, Germany, and the Cherokee Nation, and my wife is a blond New Englander whose American ancestry stretches back to the *Mayflower.*

I nodded and smiled, a proud papa. "My daughter is from here, from Kunming," I said.

An awkward and familiar silence followed. John appeared to be grappling with conflicted feelings. Most Chinese were grateful to meet a Westerner who had adopted one of the millions of girls who fill the orphanages from Heilong to Hainan, but he also appeared to have a tinge of guilt for the fact that we are needed. After looking at Liza's picture for a few seconds, John smiled and offered what I'd come to know as a standard Chinese response. "Lucky American girl," he said.

I answered with what had become my typical but heartfelt comeback. "No, we're the lucky ones."

Another moment of silence broke up when my tee time rolled around. A lovely young teenage girl interrupted us with a polite smile, nod, and a wave to follow her. It was time to play.

"This is Cindy," John said. "She is your caddie today."

I knew the girl's name wasn't Cindy, just as John's mother didn't name him after a New Testament apostle. This was something I'd come to expect and accept in China, one that saved me the embarrassment of mispronouncing names at every turn. What I hadn't quite come to grips with was the caddy situation. All of China's caddies, from those found at the best resorts to the ones who toil at the upstart courses in the countryside, are women— girls, really, some as young as fourteen years old.

"*Ní hǎo,*" Cindy said, Chinese for good morning.

"*Ní hǎo, hěn gāoxing rènshi nǐ.*" I loved showing off the few Mandarin phrases I'd picked up.

Cindy shook my hand and giggled like a typical teenager in the presence of a middle-aged man intent on embarrassing himself.

"Enjoy your round," John said as he bid us good day.

I was sure I would. Then I took one final glance at the picture of my daughter, smiling and happy, clutching the hem of her April Cornell dress in one hand and hugging her favorite Gap pillow with the other, not a care in the world beyond her afternoon ice cream and the thirty minutes of *SpongeBob* we let her watch every day. When I put my wallet away and looked up, I saw Cindy break into a trot, lugging my golf bag and all its contents up an eighteen-degree incline to the first tee.

Now it was my turn to wince with the pangs of guilt.

I'd never been to China before adopting my daughter, and had never bothered to learn much about the place. Like a lot of Americans who choose to adopt from China, my decision was purely selfish: I wanted a healthy girl with no infant drug problems and no birth mother who could show up a decade down the road, Gloria Allred at her side, claiming to be off crack and raring to resume her parenting duties.

Two years and two thousand documents later, Debbie and I got a call from our agent in Houston. "Congratulations," he said. "She's a beautiful little girl."

I have biological children, five boys in fact—four from my first marriage and a son with Debbie, and I was present for the birth of each. After adopting a child, I can say, without question, that the feelings I had when I first laid eyes on my daughter dwarfed anything (especially the hyperventilating anxiety) that I felt in the delivery room. Not only do you go through all the great feelings that come with becoming a parent again, you get a double whammy when you realize that you've rescued a kid from a life of poverty or possibly worse. Prostitution is a booming industry in China. Orphans are turned out of the government institutions and sent on their way at age fifteen. It's not hard to draw dark conclusions about where many of them end up.

We picked up Liza at a Kodak store. It was an open-front, well-lit establishment on a side street outside the gates of Yunnan University with plenty of disposable cameras and film on display. Like a lot of things on that first trip, the drop-off was quite a surprise. Our group, six couples from Detroit, Dallas, Richmond, Atlanta, Austin, and Providence, thought we were making yet another unscheduled group stop, each assuming some other expectant parent had forgotten his film. Most of us had already been in China for a week, sightseeing in Beijing, hiking the Great Wall, sipping tea at the Summer Palace, even checking out an Annie Leibovitz exhibit in the Forbidden City (something about seeing a black-and-white shot of the Dixie Chicks in the emperor's courtyard just didn't seem right). Then we went to Kunming where we saw the university, the zoo, the countryside, and then the Kodak store.

After milling around for a few minutes, one of the mothers asked, "Why are we here?"

Our minder and guide smiled and said, "Babies come here."

"The babies are coming here!" I shouted, pointing at the linoleum floor beside the disposable camera rack. "Here!"

Minutes later a bus pulled to the curb and six women got off, each carrying a child. All romantic notions we had of what the handover ceremony would be like were thrown out the window. I know that none of us envisioned seeing our children for the first time in a Kodak store. The surprises kept coming when the women, nannies from the Kunming orphanage, handed the children over and walked away. In our case, Liza, who was sixteen months old and able to stand on her own, was plopped onto the floor by a nanny who gave a curt wave, turned on her heel, and never looked back.

Debbie and I bawled like babies, not realizing that our daughter was in shock. Today it's hard to look at the photos of Liza from that first day. She and I look at them together often now, and I tell her about the moment I first saw her, but she's still too young to understand the impact of the moment.

The families in our group had also conjured fantasies about

the sites where our new daughters were abandoned. We all wanted to believe the birth mothers, poor, desperate, and scared, wrapped their children in swaddling clothes and laid them at the orphanage door. A tour of the sites pulverized those notions. One newborn had been put on a concrete piling under a freeway where rats the size of Chihuahuas scurried between heaps of trash. Another was found under a train trestle. When the train passed over, it sounded like an earthquake. Liza had been placed under a canopy at the Jinning government building a few miles out of town, one of the cleaner and safer abandonment sites from our group. Like most parents of children adopted out of China, we have no information on her birth parents or any other members of her family.

Minutes after the handover all the parents had an overwhelming desire to head home. Sightseeing was over. It was time to get back and start our lives with our new children. Unfortunately, we were held captive by a bureaucratic process (both Chinese Adoption Affairs and U.S. Immigration) that took ten days to complete. During that time, Debbie and I subjected a child who had never ridden in a car, eaten in a restaurant, or been on an elevator to two airline trips, three hotels, and a seemingly endless number of bus tours. Because we were a captive audience, our Chinese guides took us to every roadside tourist trap in the country. "It okay to shop here," they would say, "these shops owned by the government, so the quality very good." This sparked a torrent of laughter from the tour bus, much to the confused chagrin of the guides, who were simply reading from a script.

One unscripted moment came as we were driving back from some theme park or other. The guide and driver stopped the bus on the side of the road near a small mud-hut village with roaring fires and open sewers. "You have been staying in the best hotels and eating at the best restaurants," the guide said. "Now you should see how most of the country lives."

The streets were dirt, and the roofs were covered with drying corn cobs. No running water or electricity in sight, nor did I have any luck spotting a pair of shoes among the dozens of residents who rushed out to greet us. I spied one pig that looked like it had missed a few meals. The animal was locked in a pen between two dirt-floor dwellings from which no fewer than six pairs of human eyes watched my every move.

As we were leaving, I saw a young boy peek around the corner of one of the shacks. He looked to be about six. From a distance, I guessed that the clothes he wore were at least five times his age, but they appeared clean given the circumstances. I winked and waved at the boy, who put a hand over his mouth to hide a smile. Then he returned my wave and ran out of sight.

No one said a word on the ride back to our four-star hotel.

By the time we picked up Liza's passport and visa in Guang-zhou—the province in Southeastern China where 90 percent of the golf clubs and 100 percent of the Barbie dolls are made—we were frazzled, impatient, and dying for a hot dog and fries.

Once clear of Chinese airspace on our flight from Hong Kong to Chicago, my wife turned to me and said, "I don't care if we ever go back."

I nodded and said, "It will be a while, that's for sure."

———————

"A while" turned out to be two years. By the time a friend who knew the story of our adoption connected me with the travel company, the trauma of our first trip had faded. It hadn't been so bad after all, we decided, especially in light of the daughter we gained. So, when I got the invitation, I said, "Sure, I'd love to go, especially to play golf." At the time I didn't know China had more than a couple of courses, but the golf was secondary: I wanted to return to my daughter's birthplace and view the country again, this time with a relaxed heart and more dispassionate eyes.

There are three hundred courses open for play in China and another hundred under construction, not big numbers by American standards, but huge when you consider that the first course in China since the Cultural Revolution didn't open until 1985. Arnold Palmer, the designer of that first course, tells a great story that sums up China's golf evolution. "We moved approximately four hundred thousand yards of dirt, not a great amount by today's course-design standards, but still a healthy earth-moving project," Arnie says with a grin. "What I didn't know was that every ounce of dirt and rock would be moved by hand. When I went for a site visit, I saw thousands of Chinese workers with shovels and burlap sacks who had moved the better part of a half-million yards of earth. It was unbelievable. They would come upon a boulder and attack it in a swarm, beating it with picks until it was gravel. Then they'd scoop the gravel into their bags by hand and move on.

"One of the workers gave me his straw hat. He couldn't believe that I would be out there without a hat on, I guess. I didn't want to take it, but my translator told me it would be an insult to turn it down, so I put this big Chinese straw hat on my head. Then I felt around in my pocket for something to give to the guy in return. All I had was a golf ball, so I gave it to him. The guy tried to take a bite out of the cover. I said, 'No, you don't eat it.' That's when it dawned on me that the men building our golf course had no idea what golf was."

Twenty years later the game is still in its infancy in China, but the nation's passion for the game is at full speed. The courses are some of the most immaculately conditioned in the world, which makes sense when you consider the labor-intensive nature of golf course maintenance. The more workers you have, the more you're able to manicure a course. China has plenty of workers.

They also have some fantastic caddies: The girls.

Thousands of years of Asian tradition and culture dictate that women fill most of the service roles (you'll be hard-pressed to find a male barber in China). Historically, these jobs paid lower, and were a few rungs down on the social ladder. But now with the golf explosion, not only can female caddies free themselves from the drudgery of the rice paddies, but one girl in the caddy corps can quadruple a typical family income. Far from being menial jobs for slackers or kids trying to break into the workforce, caddy jobs are coveted positions in China, a responsibility the girls take very seriously.

The first stop on our trip was Hainan Island, a tropical retreat that, thirty years ago, was a military staging area, a desolate, hot holding pen for Chinese soldiers who were hanging around on the off chance that Ho Chi Minh's little skirmish didn't go as planned.

Now, it's like Maui on steroids, complete with five-star Sheratons, Marriotts, Hiltons, and Westins. As the plane was landing at Haikou airport, one of the other guys in our group (three golf writers and a couple of PGA pros) said, "Isn't this the place where that U.S. spy plane went down?"

Hainan Island is, indeed, best known in America as the place where a U.S. spy plane made an emergency landing, sparking an international incident for a couple of weeks. We decided that we wouldn't mention the incident to our hosts; no need to bring up unfortunate mishaps when you're having a good time.

We weren't on the ground five minutes when the guy who handled our ground transportation grinned and said, "You know Hainan, spy plane go down here."

After one night on the island I wondered why our spies needed to look things over from twenty-five thousand feet when they could have checked into the Marriott and gotten in a few holes of golf. They wouldn't have stood out. The resorts, of which there are many, are supersized on a scale that often borders on silly. Perry Dye and Colin Montgomerie have designed adjacent courses in Haikou, the former surrounded by condo clusters that would make a South Florida real estate developer blush, and the latter sporting a clubhouse that looks like something built by a sheikh in Abu Dhabi.

It didn't take long to realize that China was a golf course architect's dream come true. Every course is unlike anything built in America since the words "environmental impact" entered the lexicon. Want to lop the top off a mountain to build a tee? Sure, go ahead. Think it would be great to build an island green in the

South China Sea? Go for it. Need a thousand skilled and underpaid rock masons to create a stacked-stone retaining wall to hold up one of your fairways? Not a problem. One of the courses, Yalong Bay, a Robert Trent Jones Jr. design that has hosted a European PGA Tour event, is surrounded by incandescent lights and open for play until midnight.

My favorite caddy was a girl named Lu Chen, an eighteen-year-old from Dongyu Island who hasn't stopped smiling since she learned to walk. Unlike many of the caddies, who take their role as service-provider dangerously close to indentured servitude—head down, voice low, two steps behind your master—Lu Chen stuck out her hand, looked me in the eye, and introduced herself in broken English as we strolled toward the first tee at Boao Golf Club in Sanya. I could tell she was an athlete from the handshake, one of those straight-out-of-the-vise grips usually reserved for linebackers or truck drivers.

She also ran, golf clubs in tow, from the moment we teed off until the second we stepped onto the final green. She ran from the tee boxes to the fairways (or rough, depending on where my shots landed). She had everybody's yardages calculated by the time we got there. She ran from the fairways to the greens, where she cleaned our golf balls, repaired our ball marks and any left by others, and read our putts before we lumbered our overweight behinds onto the apron. After the putts fell, she put the flag in the hole and ran to the next tee, where she calculated wind direction and target line before we arrived.

Finally, I asked, "Lu Chen, do the words 'saunter' or 'stroll' translate into Chinese?"

"Saucer?"

"No, saunter."

She giggled and smiled, but had no clue what I was saying.

"How about 'walk'?"

Recognition sparked across her face. "Yes, yes," she said, patting me on the back. "You walk." And that was how it was going to be: I walk, she runs.

She ran into places I wouldn't send my golden retriever. The Boao course, designed by a local architect whose name is unpronounceable and therefore cannot be phonetically butchered here, is replete with natural vegetation, much of it bordering the fairways near the landing areas. It reminded me of the tiger scene in *Apocalypse Now*. You wouldn't venture into most of the brush without a machete and a shotgun, but Lu Chen ran headlong into whatever jungle my bad swing found, despite my protests. I finally said, "Lu Chen, I have plenty of golf balls, and money to buy more if we run out." That didn't translate either. On she went, running into the bush and coming out with my ball and half a dozen others. It put enormous pressure on me to hit fairways.

A couple of holes after one of her ball-hawking excursions, Lu Chen saved my life. We were walking across a footbridge that crossed a small stream when she casually pointed to the ground and said, "Watch out cobra."

I did one of those flying Michael Jordan leaps that would have looked great in a Nike ad. When I hit the ground I said, "Did you say cobra?"

She pointed, and sure enough, coiled near the exit to the bridge was the first cobra I had seen outside the confines of a zoo.

I grabbed Lu Chen by the shoulders and said, "Lu Chen, we are not looking for any more golf balls. No more."

She smiled, nodded, and said, "More golf ball, yes."

After that we got along great. When I asked a question she didn't understand, like, "How far to clear the bunkers?" she shook her head, and I drew a schematic on the back of a scorecard. "Here to here, how far?"

She would nod with recognition and say, "Two hundred twenty yard."

During one of the few moments when I got her to slow down enough to chat, I learned that Lu Chen lives in a two-room house (or hut, depending on your frame of reference) with six other people. She has been caddying since she was fifteen, and plays golf in the few odd minutes when caddies are allowed on the course. She is the Chinese equivalent of a senior in high school, but when I asked about her plans for the future, she looked at me as though I'd grown two heads. That's when I realized that I was looking at her future, and was too naive to know it.

I squinted into the breeze. I wanted to put Lu Chen in my luggage and smuggle her back to America where I could give her a bag full of clubs, send her outside and say, "Be a girl. Enjoy yourself. Have a good time."

When we finished, after she had cleaned my clubs and slapped my hand when I tried to help, I tipped her 150 yuan, the equivalent of about $20 in America and somewhere close to a half-month's pay in Hainan province. When I saw tears well up in her eyes I had to turn my back before she saw mine.

As we loaded our bags into the van and prepared to set out for our next destination, Lu Chen stood on the curb with her fellow caddies, waved, and chanted her obviously memorized salutation: "Goodbye, and good luck."

I couldn't hold back the tears after that. "No, Lu Chen," I thought, "good luck to you."

I couldn't shake that memory as I played the Mountain Course at Spring City with Cindy, who did a magnificent job trudging up and down the hilly terrain, giving directions, and pulling the right club for every shot. By the time we reached the 205-yard par-three thirteenth, Cindy knew my game well enough to hand me a five-iron.

I hit a good shot, but my eyesight is so bad I haven't seen a five-iron come down in ten years. "That might be close," I said.

Then Cindy began jumping up and down and shouting, *"Xion zhou! Xion zhou!"*

"Sorry, Cindy, I have no idea what you're saying," I said.

Another caddy in our group translated: "She say, 'It in the hole.'"

Cindy was right. It was, indeed, in the hole, the third hole-in-one of my golfing life, but far and away the most meaningful. Not only was it my first ace outside the United States, it came in the town where my daughter was born, the town I had cursed during my initial visit, the one I had sworn I would not visit again "for a while." Now I was being treated like a mini-emperor. Cindy couldn't stop smiling as she told every maintenance worker and marshal on the course about my shot.

Word traveled fast. When we arrived back at the clubhouse

the entire caddy staff, forty young ladies, lined the curb and cheered my arrival so enthusiastically that I had to look over my shoulder to make sure Britney Spears's tour bus hadn't pulled in. Then the caddy master grabbed the scorecard from my hand and waved it to the crowd, prompting another round of wild applause.

John, the general manager, joined the chorus, showering me with gifts. Among them, a cell phone that only works in China, a round-trip airline ticket from Kunming, China, to Seoul, South Korea (for those occasions when I've got a couple of days to kill in Southeast Asia), and, most ironic of all, two cases of Chinese Coca-Cola.

"You know I live in Atlanta," I said to John after I thanked him.

"Yes, yes, Coca-Cola," he said.

I bowed, and offered my most heartfelt *"Xiexie"* to everyone. It was the least I could do for the most celebrated swing I've ever made, and a shot I will savor for the rest of my life. Not only was I the first American to make an ace on the thirteenth hole at Spring City, I was the first Westerner, a fact verified by a stone sign on the tee listing every golfer who has accomplished this feat. Today, my name appears beneath that of Yang Dong Hyuk and Lee Hong Suk.

As I flew out of Shanghai two days later, I tried to reflect on everything I'd seen and done. No matter how much you read and hear about the explosive Chinese economy, until you see it, you have no idea what 18-percent-a-year GDP growth looks like. There are places where construction cranes atop partially developed high-rises litter the landscape as far as you can see in every direction. Cars, once a luxury for the rich, make every road in the country look like a Los Angeles freeway on Friday afternoon. And the middle class is beginning to blossom. Kids with iPods don't quite outnumber panhandlers, but I saw a lot of Wranglers and designer sunglasses.

Now, I can't wait to take my daughter back to the city of her birth, to show her the culture, and the people, and the beauty of China. I will show her the new buildings and roads, the new golf courses and hotels, and I will introduce her to the caddies, telling her the stories of the girls I met there. I will explain how many of the caddies in China are learning to play golf, just as she is learning to play on our course back home. I will show her the orphanage where she lived, and the Kodak store where we first saw her, and I will point to the changes being made in China. And I will show her the rock on the thirteenth tee at the Mountain Course at Spring City, the one with her daddy's name engraved on it: a stone fixture commemorating one golf swing that will forever tie me to the land where her life—and our lives together—began.

SIX

Doonbeg-doggle

(or How Not to Represent Your Country)

The international portion of my odyssey didn't end in Asia, although it should have. How do you top a hole-in-one in the town of your adopted daughter's birth? You can't, and you're an idiot if you try. But intelligence and rationality never stopped me before, so when my friend and fellow sports writer Furman Bisher asked me to join him for a little golf in Ireland, I didn't spend a lot of introspective time pondering where such a journey might rate on my cool-things-in-life card.

"Doonbeg, Buddy Darby's golf club on the southwest coast, is hosting something called the 'Writer's Cup,' a match-play thing with golf writers from the U.S. and the E.U.," Furman said. "I'm captaining the U.S. team. I'm hoping you'll be my captain's pick."

Not wanting to look like a dog going after a porterhouse, I said, "Well, Furman, let me think about it . . . Okay, yes."

"Great," he said. "You'll be getting some info from the marketing people at Doonbeg."

Okay, this wasn't like saying, "You'll be getting a welcome packet from the U.S. Olympic Committee," or "Congratulations, you've made the World Cup team." The "Writer's Cup" wasn't sanctioned by anyone other than the developer footing the bill. But it was as close to representing my country in a sporting event as I was ever going to get, so I saluted smartly, thanked my captain, and whistled John Philip Sousa tunes while packing for another transoceanic boondoggle.

The well-trodden term for audacious excursions like this is "FAM trip," a breezy abbreviation for "familiarization trip," which is, itself, code for "expensive bribe." My brethren in travel media will excommunicate me for breaking the rich and long-standing code of silence, but (shock of shocks) the media actually accept freebies from our sources, our subjects . . . hell, we take stuff from everybody.

For those young ideological innocents who harbor dreamy notions about the nobility of journalism, let me be the villain who says there is no Santa. We, the professionals of the press, the only private-sector grunts whose jobs are ostensibly protected by the First Amendment, are in our hearts and souls a gaggle of freeks. The only differentiator among us—whether we are the pious voices of network news, or grungy travel hacks slogging out a thousand words for the latest mag to put a half-naked hottie on the cover—is the sliding scale that has always existed in the world's oldest profession: "How much?"

In the case of golf writers, the price tag starts at free food and alcohol. One of the oldest jokes among tournament organizers is that if you want good ink you'd better stock the golf writers' favorite beers, Free and Free Lite. Ever wonder why the Masters is always written about so glowingly? Frank Deford shared the secret with me a decade ago, when he bluntly stated, "Nobody who covers the World Series longs to play center field for the Dodgers. No theater critic expects to get a good role on Broadway. But trust me, kid, every guy who covers the Masters writes about it with the thought in mind that if he toes the party line, someday he might get an invitation to play there."

If that doesn't deflate your Robert-Redford-as-Bob-Woodward view of the fourth estate, it gets worse. Golf travel journalists not only don't flinch at free air travel, lodging, food, drink, entertainment, green fees, and caddies, but a lot of the more pugnacious writers take offense when they aren't given first-class airline seats and a couple of bottles of wine in their complimentary suites. Most major magazines and newspapers insist that their reporters pay for junkets—journalistic integrity and all—but "discounts" are acceptable, or at least unquestioned.

Find a sports reporter who has paid rack rate green fees for every round of golf he's played in the last twelve months and I'll show you someone who doesn't get out very often. The big question among golf journalists these days is not "How much is this going to cost?" but "How good is it going to be?"

In the case of Doonbeg and the Writer's Cup, the answer was: so good that even the most cynical scribes were blushing as they said things like "This is unbelievable."

We were in County Clare to "familiarize" ourselves with the new lodge at Doonbeg, a palatial compound sitting a shanked sand wedge from the shores of the Atlantic. Built by Americans

Buddy Darby and his cousin Leonard Long (the same wizards who bought Kiawah Island in 1988 and finagled a Ryder Cup on their land before a golf course was built), the digs at Doonbeg were so over the top they would have made Richard de Clare blink.

The lodge itself was a giant clubhouse, complete with golf shop, pub, members' bar, formal and informal dining rooms, locker rooms (separate for members and guests), a spa, and as an added bonus, fifteen member-owned suites that can be rented out from time to time.

"Buddy and I don't know much, but we know quality," Leonard said.

It would have been easy to dismiss that proclamation as just so much developer blarney. I felt like saying, "Yada, yada, yada, where's the bar." Then I went to my suite where my wardrobe was lying on the bed along with a note that said, "Welcome to Doonbeg. Here are your uniforms for the week."

At the first tee (five steps from the front door of the lodge) I met up with our team captain, Furman Bisher. Furman was one of the true legends in sports journalism, perhaps the only guy in the world who saw Cy Young pitch, Gene Tunney box, and was there when Tiger Woods won his four straight majors. Furman played golf with Jimmy Demaret (and forced the former Masters winner to birdie the last hole to beat him), had Bobby Jones's home phone number in his Rolodex, spent a weekend in Sam Snead's guest room, covered every Super Bowl, and has been to every Masters and Kentucky Derby since Truman beat Dewey. At eighty-seven, he was down to two columns a week, and was still one of the most read sports writers in the country, a fact that drove his editors bonkers.

"You know, they tried to tell me I couldn't come to this thing," Furman said with a scowl. "Editor was giving me the stink eye, saying that if Buddy was paying for anything I couldn't go."

"What did you tell him?" I asked.

"I told him I was going. I gave my word to these people. I said, 'If you want to pay for it, fine. But I'm not going back on my word.'"

"How'd that go over?"

He smiled and said, "I'm here. I just wish I could get out on the course with you today." Furman rotated his torso in an attempt to stretch, and said, "I just can't turn the way I used to."

I was sitting behind Furman on the flight to Ireland, so I knew that he hadn't slept all night, and that his body clock was telling him it was four in the morning.

"Furman, when I'm your age I hope I know my name, and am able to sit upright to take nourishment."

"I don't know. When your mind's willing but your body won't respond it's frustrating."

"When do you turn eighty-eight?"

"Five months. No rush."

Before I could comment further on Furman's advanced years, two other members of our stellar American squad showed up. Larry Olmsted, a Vermont resident and the kind of golf freak who made me look like a piker, was squeezing the Writer's Cup between a tour of the coastal resorts of Spain and a Parisian cheese tasting near the Musée d'Orsay. It was his third trip to Ireland in twelve months. "Just glad I was able to work it in," he said.

The other fellow, who I learned would be occupying the

second bedroom in my thousand-square-foot suite, was a six-foot, nine-inch giant with a goatee and shock of wavy white hair that made him look like the bastard love child of Barbara Bush and Lurch from *The Addams Family*.

"Turk Pipkin," he said, extending a hand the size of a catcher's mitt.

"Did you say Kirk?" I asked.

"No, Turk."

"Oh, like turd with a K."

Thus were the beginnings of a new and consequential friendship, one that far outlasted our tenure as comrades on Furman Bisher's Team America. I had no idea who my suitemate was other than the fact that he was a big, funny guy who lived in Austin and wrote for *Texas Monthly*. It wasn't until a couple of days later, as we were standing in the pub waiting for the Guinness to develop a proper head, that one of our fellow drinkers sidled up to the bar and said, "Excuse me, aren't you that actor on *The Sopranos*?"

I started to say no, but realized the guy was talking to Turk.

"I am," Turk said, and he shook the guy's hand and introduced himself.

"I knew I recognized you," the guy said. "I love your character. You gonna be back this season?"

"Not sure how many episodes, but I'll make a few appearances," Turk said.

After the sycophants bought Turk a round and trotted off to tell their friends about their brush with fame, I said, "You're an actor?"

"Did you think I'd let all this charm and wit go to waste?"

"I know I'm culturally illiterate, but what have you done?"

"Well, I was a stand-up comic with Rodney Dangerfield and Harry Anderson, and then got into movies and television."

"What'd you play on *The Sopranos?* Jeez, that's a show I actually watch. I can't believe I didn't recognize you."

"Aaron Arkaway, Janice's evangelical narcoleptic songwriting ex-boyfriend."

"You were the guy who fell asleep at the Thanksgiving dinner table holding the carving knife in the turkey!"

"My finest hour."

"Didn't I see you on one of the recent ones after Tony got shot?"

"Yeah, I was sitting in the hospital waiting room. It was funny because they called and said they wanted me for the scene, but they didn't give me any more detail. So, I show up and the wardrobe girl hands me what was, without a doubt, the most offensive T-shirt I'd ever seen, and says 'This is what you're going to wear.'"

"What was on it?"

"It was a regular T-shirt, but it said, 'Terry Schiavo Vigil. You Go Girl!'"

"Oh my god."

"Yeah; that one offended everybody."

If Turk took offense at my having no idea who he was, he didn't show it. Later that night I Googled his name and saw that he had been in *The Alamo* and *Friday Night Lights* with Billy Bob Thornton, and had costarred with Willie Nelson and Kris Kristofferson in *A Pair of Aces.* He also cowrote Willie's book, *The Tao of Willie.* The other book of his I recognized was a humorous memoir of breaking 80 at Pebble Beach to honor his dead father called *The Old Man and the Tee.* I had read that book without paying much attention to the author. Since he was sleeping thirty feet away from me, I chose not to say, "Hey, I even read one of your books and didn't know who you were."

In our final practice round before teeing it up for our country, Turk and I agreed that calling this one "over the top" didn't come close. When the caddies met us on the first tee in white jumpsuits with our names embroidered on their backs, I finally said, "Okay, this is getting embarrassing."

Then the starter called us. I expected the standard "Get your butts in gear; keep up with the group in front of you; and no doddling at the refreshment stand" speech. Instead, a smiling Irishman in a tweed jacket and touring cap handed us our scorecards, opened a humidor, and said, "What we smoking today, gents?"

"I'll have a Cuban Cohiba, thank you," I said before he changed his mind.

"You don't screw around, do you?" Turk said.

"Not as long as they're offering."

The starter smiled and said, "We'll have sandwiches and some beverages out to you shortly, and there's water and fruit on the tees."

"What, no massages at the turn?" I said.

"You're scheduled for one in the spa after your round. I hope that's all right."

"Shut up and tee off before they give us the key to the village," Turk said.

The golf course was fantastic if you like links golf, a brand of the game that is obliged to include blind tee shots, bunkers that look like dried wells or abandoned mine shafts, knee-deep wispy rough, and hellacious wind.

I love it. From the first moment I put a peg in the ground at Portmarnock in Dublin, to the two weeks I spent as a guest of the R&A playing the eight courses of the Open Championship rotation, to the quick eighteens I've played at places like St. Annes Old Links, Gullane No. 1, North Berwick, and Kingsbarn before heading out to watch Tiger and the gang tee off in the oldest championship in the world, links golf, in my book, tops all others. I love the bounces, the stark terrain, the creative shotmaking, and the mile-long putts. There's nothing like hitting three-wood into a par three one day and having a seven-iron from the same tee the next. And there is no feeling in the world like standing on a windswept tee surrounded by dunes and gorse, next to the lapping waves of a frigid sea.

Having experienced it all, I can say that the best links golf in Scotland is in Ireland and the best in England is, well, not very good. Nothing in the Kingdom can match the links of Lahinch, Portmarnock, Waterville, or Ballybunion, where the target for your opening tee shot is a headstone in an adjacent graveyard. Doonbeg, a mere infant in the world of links golf (having been designed by Greg Norman in the current millennium) is fast moving up that list.

"Has anybody been here before?" I asked my American teammates milling around the first tee.

"I have," Furman said. "I came for the grand opening, but it's not the same golf course it was then. When Norman played the inaugural round the fairways were so narrow he had trouble breaking eighty. He was standing right here on this tee talking about what a great treat it was to have this beautiful piece of land, and Buddy Darby leaned over my shoulder and whispered, 'Two years from now, he won't recognize the place.' "

"How long ago was that?"

"Five years, and he was right. It's a lot better golf course now."

I put it in the great category. Twice, I had to aim a hundred yards away from where I wanted the ball to end up because of the wind and the bounces my caddy assured me we were going to get. We measured one downwind drive at 400 yards, and one well-struck into-the-wind tee shot that flew a total of 170. It was exactly what links golf should be.

Turk didn't have as much fun. With a slow and deliberate takeaway, the big man caught the driver yips on the second tee, and proceeded to hit the next ten tee shots an average of fifty yards each. His shot of choice was a low, smothering hook, the kind of shot that would have ricocheted off the shank if he'd been hitting an iron. The ball never got above waist high, which might have been okay had Doonbeg's tees not been surrounded by waist-high grass dunes.

After Turk's third tee shot spattered through the high stuff like a lawn mower choking on leaves, my caddy, Hugh, said "Shit, he's hit it in the dick weeds again."

"You mean duck weeds?" I asked.

"No, we don't have duck weeds. Around here if it grows dick high it's a dick weed."

Hugh was what American tourists refer to as "local color." With no filter between brain and tongue, he was not bashful about sharing his opinions with every member of the group regardless of whether or not we wanted it. When Larry Olmsted backed away from a shot to check the wind and reconsider his club selection, Hugh stormed past him and said, "Ohfurfooksake, hit the ball and be on your way."

Once, after finally getting a tee shot airborne, Turk said, "Wow, where has that been?"

Hugh answered, "I don't know, but hopefully it'll go back there. Your ball's in the shit."

Somewhere on the back nine, after Turk had lost a dozen balls and Larry was oh-for-forever in fairways hit, I said, "Do you guys play much?"

"I've been doing a lot of resort travel lately, and haven't had a lot of time for golf," Larry said. "I was in Spain, and I went home, where I did nothing but work around the house, then I flew here. I'll go back home for two days, and then to France to eat cheese for a week."

"Why not go straight from here to France?"

"I have a wife who'd like to see me," he said. "Plus, I've got a friend getting married, and I have to be there for his wedding. It's one of those big social affairs. I'd be in huge trouble if I missed it."

"Expensive?"

"Obscene."

"Tell him he's wasting his money," I said. "My first wedding was a huge church deal with tuxedos, bridesmaids, big cake, music, champagne, the whole bit. The marriage was a complete disaster. Second time around my wife and I got married by a midget riverboat captain in Chattanooga at seven in the morning. Whole thing cost me three hundred dollars including a breakfast reception with biscuits and gravy. That marriage has worked out great."

"They like to be called 'little people.'"

"What about you, Turk?" I yelled to the head bobbing around in the dick weeds left of the fairway. "You married?"

"Yeah, I'm married to a midget riverboat captain. Sometimes he lets me toot his horn."

Buddy Darby continued to pile on the goodies, setting us up with full-body massages, sauna, steam, and hot tub treatments, followed by a seven-course meal and free rein of the wine list. But the next day we got down to business. Dressed in matching red shirts and blue slacks, team USA stumbled out to the first tee where each of us was expected to do our nation proud.

Sure, it was a boondoggle for journalists, an expensive excuse to get a bunch of travel hacks to say nice things about a golf course that didn't need our endorsement to be great. But when the words "Now on the tee, representing the United States" came out of the starter's mouth, I, and many of my teammates, went dry as Alabama cotton.

My experience was the worst, because I was the first player off. Every employee and member in the vicinity plus members of both teams stood by to watch. When my name came after "representing the United States" I think the crowd applauded, but I couldn't differentiate the claps from the pounding of my heart.

I had been nervous on the first tee before. When I played in college, every time my name was called in state amateurs and club championships I felt butterflies. During local U.S. Open qualifying I had to take several deep breaths before the first swing, even though I knew my chances of advancing were slim. But this time, with the whole of America to represent, I sucked hard before finding a single molecule of air.

I actually touched the bill of my cap and nodded to the applauding gallery. Then my brain screamed, "You moron. Do you realize how idiotic that looked?" But I kept going, reaching in my pocket for a tee and finding every penny, key, cell phone, crumpled receipt, and marble I'd collected since leaving home.

After an interminable couple of seconds where I heard nothing but a cough from the gallery and the *ka-thud, ka-thud, ka-thud* of my 200-beat-a-minute heart, I finally felt the distinct needle prick of a golf tee. Satisfied that I hadn't wasted too much time, I jerked the wooden peg from my pocket. And my phone, room key, two golf balls, and sixty-four cents in coinage spilled out onto the ground. I might have been able to cover, but when one cab and two parking receipts fluttered away like confetti at a convention, I knew there was no escape.

"Take your time," I heard someone say through a snicker.

Poor Furman, the oldest guy in the gallery by at least two decades, leapt forward to help gather the spilled change.

"Don't worry, Furman, I'll get it in a second," I said. Oh god, when was this going to end?

Breath and balance were rare commodities as I bent over and put my ball on the tee. I gripped my driver and went through the same pre-shot routine I'd done millions of times in my life. Then I stepped up to the ball, waggled the club, and told myself not to vomit. I tried to focus on a target, but everything beyond the end of the tee box was a blur. After three or four more waggles, I finally pulled the trigger.

It was the kind of move you might see if lightning struck a tree in the middle of a player's backswing, the quickest thrash this side of a Singapore caning.

I never saw the ball, but the starter said, "Ooh, you better watch that one," which is never a good sign.

No applause. No chatter. Just a few murmurs from the back row, which included someone saying "One down." After another infinite couple of seconds I was off the tee, handing my driver to Hugh. Only then did I say, "Where'd it go?"

In his own calm and encouraging way, Hugh said, "You're in the shit."

I calmed down after the first tee, and for the next three days played well and had a wonderful time. And what was not to like? Buddy turned out to be a wine snob, so we drank nothing but the good stuff, the kind with triple-digit price tags. We smoked fine Cubans every day, drank pints after our rounds, and enjoyed massages every evening before dinner.

Out of six possible points in the Writer's Cup, I won three and lost three, a very respectable .500 split that allowed me to go home happy. One other member of our team, Hunki Yun, the editor of a magazine aptly titled *LINKS*, also went three-and-three. Other than that, we, as Americans are wont to do in international golf competitions, got creamed. Turk and Larry both went oh-for-six, much to the consternation of our captain, who took the competition to heart.

"I can't believe there weren't any more decent players," Furman said to me afterward. "Other than you and Hunki Yun, who I thought was a woman before I met him, we didn't have anybody who could play a lick. I thought we'd put up a little better fight."

I put my arm around him and said, "Don't worry, Furman, we'll get them in two years."

"I hope I'm around to get invited back."

"So do I, friend," I said, knowing Furman would be ninety before either of us got another invitation to this event. "I'll be on your team as long as you'll have me."

SEVEN

Green Flag Golfer

(or Don't Hit Driver at the Driver!)

One of the greatest things about sports writing (in addition to the lavish meals, five-star complimentary accommodations, and swag bags that rival those doled out at awards shows) is the great golf you can play while attending other events. In addition to playing great links courses while covering the British Open, I've slipped out to Winged Foot, Quaker Ridge, Ridgewood, and Brooklawn while PGA Tour players were tearing up Westchester Country Club. The morning of Super Bowl XXXIX I played the TPC at Sawgrass before heading down to Alltel Stadium. Sugar Bowl morning I was across the river cutting a five-wood into the eighteenth green at English Turn, and during the Sunday break of the Championships at Wimbledon, I was at Wentworth seeing how many holes I could get in before dark.

Not all the courses have been world-class. Brookside Golf Course in Pasadena is a fine, flat public facility, but you don't find yourself breaking out the camera and thumbing through the thesaurus for superlatives as you play it. The course's biggest benefit is that it sits right next door to the Rose Bowl. Quail Chase, a lovely but less-than-spectacular public course in Louisville, is a great place to spend Sunday after the Kentucky Derby. It's only fifteen minutes from Churchill Downs, and Louisville is beautiful in May.

My worst golf experience on the road to another sporting event was at the Pocono Golf Club, a nine-hole par 32 course with rubber mats for tees, greens no bigger than the hood of your car, and fairways that are mown every other week or when Euley Padgett brings the tractor back after plowing his field. A friend and I were on our way to Long Pond, Pennsylvania, home of the Pocono Raceway and the Pennsylvania 500, when I spotted a fairway and green on the side of the road.

"Want to stop?" I asked.

"Are you serious?"

"We've got clubs in the trunk."

"Do you want to?"

"No reason to let it pass," I said as I performed an illegal U-turn and whipped into the entrance.

The clubhouse looked like the Ingalls cabin on *Little House on the Prairie,* and the proprietor, a man with grease on his T-shirt and jeans, one hand petting his Lab while the other worked a toothpick between a couple of bicuspids, seemed stunned to see us on his doorstep. When he hopped up, the dog greeted my buddy by sniffing his crotch.

"You're going to love the course," he said as he handed us a cart key attached to the end of a two-by-four.

"Love" was too strong a word, just as "hate" wouldn't have been appropriate either. We were, after all, playing golf. The gas-powered golf cart sounded like a '69 Dodge Dart with a hole in the muffler. My friend bounced it down the dirt path of the first hole, kicking up a cloud of dust in our wake. "I'm not sure we're going to love this," he said.

"It's golf, baby. What's not to love?"

We loved it until we struggled to find the second hole. After driving around in circles for a minute or two, we finally arrived at the second tee, a three-by-three strip of Astroturf nailed to the ground in the middle of a stand of pine trees. It would have looked like a wildlife viewing stand if it wasn't ten feet of brush and briars from State Route 15. Just beyond the artificial teeing ground, we noticed a sign in the forest that read, "You are Responsible for Damage Caused by Your Golf Ball (example: automobiles)."

"I have to have that sign," my friend said.

"I don't think it's for sale."

"You think they'll miss it?"

"I think they've probably got a few more lying around."

"It's not secured. What do you think?"

"We could always pull it up, leave it on the side of the road, and pick it up on our way out," I said. I was the more experienced petty thief in our twosome, even though it had been almost a quarter century since I'd stolen a sign. The last one had been an entry sign at Hollow Creek Country Club that read: "Whites Only." Not only did I want that one for posterity's sake ("look, kids, people really did this sort of thing") I wanted the old bastards at Hollow Creek to have to pay to replace it. But this was different.

We were middle-aged men at a course we'd stumbled onto by accident, plotting the theft of a cheap, rusted sign strictly for humor's sake.

"Think we'll get away with it?" my friend asked.

"We're in the middle of the woods," I said.

At this point stronger, more principled men would have laughed off the idea and moved along. We did not qualify. I pulled up the sign and left it on the shoulder of the highway. As we left the premises, I stopped the rental car and popped the trunk while my friend hopped out and grabbed the sign—a classic smash and grab job. We felt like Butch and Sundance.

Not that it justifies our thievery, but I donated enough golf balls at Pocono to more than make up for the cost of the cheap sign. On one of the five par threes, the yardage marker on the Astroturf read "200 yards."

"Does that look like two hundred yards to you?" I asked my partner in crime.

"The greens are so bloody small, how could you know?"

The greens were, indeed, the smallest I had ever seen. Adding to the confusion was the fact that each of the nine flagsticks was a different height, depending on how many times it had been broken, creating a depth-perception illusion. I decided to split the difference between the marker and my gut and go with a six-iron (the club I normally hit 190 yards). The ball was still rising as it flew into the trees behind the green.

"Oh my god, you've hit it into the car park!" my friend shouted as the ball bounded through the parking lot of Ruby's Country Fried Chicken Restaurant. We lost sight of it as it hopped beneath a traffic light and a line of whizzing cars. At that instant, we both understood the significance of the sign we had stolen.

A seven-iron from the same tee produced a similar result. A nine-iron was also long. When I finally choked down on my sand wedge, I realized that the yardage at Pocono Golf Club was off by no less than 100 yards per hole. After donating half-a-dozen balls I decided they could certainly live without their precious little sign.

Example: automobiles, indeed.

As convenient as it is to play courses like Pocono, Brookside, Quail Chase, and Wentworth, none of those courses were actually in the stadiums I was going to visit. Some were close—Sawgrass Country Club is a mile from the TPC where The Players Championship is contested; the Country Club in Brookline is a fifteen-minute cab ride from Fenway—but you can't tee off on the thirteenth hole and watch batting practice at the same time.

There is only one sporting venue where you can watch the action and line up a ten-footer for birdie: the Indianapolis Motor Speedway, home of the Indy 500.

Okay, you can't actually play during the race. But folks in Indianapolis consider every practice and qualifying session to be part of the show, and you can certainly play during those. The track opens for practice the first weekend in May, and it stays open until Memorial Day Sunday when the race winner guzzles the ceremonial quart of milk. The adjacent golf course, Brickyard Crossing, is open for business throughout every practice and qualifying session right up until race weekend, which wouldn't be unusual, except that holes seven, eight, nine, and ten are routed through the track's massive infield. If you time it properly, you can catch an hour of Indy practice or qualifying while playing a leisurely eighteen.

I did exactly that.

The infield pagoda at the Speedway that houses the media center, offices, and a couple of storage closets is a shrine, and Gasoline Alley, a fine enough garage but concrete-block buildings nonetheless, is spoken about as if it were paved in gold. To think of anything other than racing while cars are on the track is akin to blasphemy. That was one of the reasons Brickyard Crossing was all but empty when I showed up to play.

I called the golf pro prior to waltzing in. Whenever you're finagling a free round, it helps to let your mark know you're coming; that way you can feel out the pro-shop hierarchy and figure out which person in the pecking order is most likely to say, "Go ahead, you're our guest today." The pro was coy on the phone, giving up nothing. I got the feeling he, too, was shocked that someone would care more about golf than monitoring lap times.

"Come on out," he said. "A single won't have any problem."

It took about two minutes to get from the infield parking lot to the golf shop, which sits in the shadows of the Turn Two grandstands. When I arrived, the place was empty save for two lone pros, one standing and one sitting, with nothing to do but dust the counter and rearrange the sweaters. Race or no race, it was hard to believe. This was a Pete Dye design, one of the best public golf courses in the country. *Golf Digest* ranked it forty-seventh among the public courses in America, and the PGA Tour thought enough of it to hold six Senior Tour events there.

As odd as it seems, the infield at the Indianapolis Motor Speedway has been home to a golf course since 1929. In those days the course was twenty-seven holes with the third nine routed through the infield. In the early sixties, the PGA Tour held an event there as part of race festivities. The Beatles even whacked a few around. The Fab Four's only golf picture was staged on one of the Speedway course's greens.

The Tour left in 1966, and the old layout wasn't attracting many new visitors. So IMS president Tony George, who, along with his sister Mary, inherited the track from their grandfather, decided to revamp the place, turn twenty-seven tired holes into eighteen eye-popping new ones. Four, not nine, holes ran through the infield, which left room for an infield racing museum and motor coach parking. Once Pete Dye was finished, Brickyard Crossing was named the best public course in Indiana.

I couldn't wait to get out there. And I was ready to pay, especially when I didn't get any warm-and-fuzzy offers from the assistant pro. Sometimes the dance of the freeloading golfer requires a bit of foreplay. I commented on the quality of the merchandise displays, asked a few probing questions about the demand for logo apparel, and delved into the background of the man behind the counter with a few "how did you get into the business" questions. But nothing seemed to work. Then I saw one of the books I had previously written on a shelf behind the counter.

"That's one of my books," I said, nodding as if I'd asked the guy to break a dollar for the vending machine.

That line always worked. I expected the pro to say something like "Really? Would you sign it for me? And, by the way, you can play as our guest today." Shameless, I know, but I had found it to be one of the greatest pickup lines in golf.

This time the guy simply grunted. The tone of his "Hmm" said it all. He believed me; he just didn't care.

"You wrote that?" a voice said from behind me.

I turned to see two heavyset guys in their thirties who had come into the shop through a different entrance. They had their golf shoes on, and it was too early for them to be finished, so I assumed they were coming to play. The one who asked the question was pointing to the book with the kind of wide-eyed sparkle I had expected out of the assistant pro.

"I did," I said, trying to ooze my best Steve McQueen cool.

"I've read that book," the guy said. Then he turned to his partner and said, "Have you read that book?"

The guy shook his head and grunted.

"It's a good book." Then back to me: "Be damned. You wrote that?"

I introduced myself—for the sake of their own protection, I'm calling them Stan and Bill—and said, "So, are you guys playing today?"

If I could keep Stan gushing about my book, maybe the assistant pro would take notice.

"Yeah, we're going out in about fifteen minutes," Stan said. "You?"

"I'm looking for a game if you've only got two."

Stan threw his hands up like he'd just won the grand prize on *Deal or No Deal.* "Sure! We'd love to have you!" Only then did he turn to Bill and say, "You okay with that?"

Bill shrugged again, and mumbled something that could have been "Sure."

"So, do you guys live here?"

"No," Stan said as he whipped out his American Express card. "We live in Michigan. We're with Ford. Down here for the month of May."

"You should be down my way at the NASCAR race, shouldn't you?" I said.

Now it was Stan's turn to shrug. "We're exploring our opportunities in open-wheel racing."

"Whatever that means," Bill chimed in.

I could tell I was going to like these two.

Having given up on the assistant, I reached for my wallet. Stan waved me off. "No, no, Ford's picking up golf today."

"Are you sure?" I said, which was better than the "Yes!" that was screaming through my temples.

"Absolutely," Stan said. "Company's broke anyway. I don't think one round of golf's gonna matter."

No doubt about it: This was going to be fun.

As a connoisseur of good golf courses I can tell you that all great designers have trademarks. Robert Trent Jones Jr. is a fan of huge flash bunkers with tongues of turf sitting right on the line that your eye tells you to hit. Tom Fazio can't go anywhere without leaving a false front or two on his greens. Ben Crenshaw moves a minimal amount of dirt and crowns his greens to put a premium on putting, while Jack Nicklaus sticks bunkers or trees in the middle of his fairways at the exact distance a normal tee shot will land. Tom Doak seems to love sidehill slopes. And the dearly departed Joe Lee built more gooseneck holes snaking around hazards than Ford sold Model Ts.

Pete Dye courses have a similarly distinct imprint. You can expect huge bunkers, some extending from tee to green, and a few pot bunkers so deep and steep you need a ladder to get in and out. Pete's greens have swoops and swirls, and his approaches always have some knob or slope that will repel a shot that isn't struck perfectly. The whole concept of the game is to reward good shots and punish bad ones, but most architects give the average- to high-handicap player a path to making bogey. Not Pete. A legitimate 25-handicap golfer, playing by the rules, will shoot somewhere between 120 and 150 on Pete's most famous course, the TPC at Sawgrass. And that assumes that the player doesn't run out of balls on the seventeenth tee. Scores at Teeth of the Dog, Pete's Dominican Republic masterpiece, are even higher.

I've played enough tough golf courses that degree of difficulty doesn't bother me much. It's nice when a good shot is rewarded, but golf, like life, isn't fair, so I don't expect glorious results every time. But if I were a high-handicapper—a player like Stan or Bill—I would have dived in front of a speeding race car before playing another Pete Dye golf course.

I knew we were in for an eventful round when Stan snap-hooked his opening shot into a waste bunker just a few yards in front of the first tee. That said, he was in far better shape than his partner. Bill took a massive swing, a gargantuan cut that began with the club wrapped around his neck on the backswing until it pointed at the ground. His knees bent like a weight lifter trying to set a clean-and-jerk record, and then sprang up on his downswing as if he were shooting a free throw. As a result, Bill set a new and until then uncharted record for the hardest golf swing to produce the shortest shot. The vicious swipe must have clipped no more than a single dimple of the ball, because it dribbled about two feet in front of him.

Having only met the man moments earlier, I struck a stoic pose and said nothing. Stan showed no such restraint. He laughed so hard he stumbled around the tee like a drunk. Pretty soon, I could hold it in no longer and joined him.

"Thanks," Bill said.

"Take a mulligan," I said. "You needed one swing to loosen up."

His second shot squirreled off into the right rough, but at least he cleared the end of the tee.

"Much better," I said.

"Be hard for it to have been worse," Stan said, which prompted another torrent of laughter.

And so it went for the first six holes. Bill plodded his way up the right-hand rough, while Stan hit more tailhooks than a Navy pilot. They both deposited a fair number of balls in Little Eagle Creek. On the sixth, Bill and I stood on the green waiting for Stan to extricate himself from one of Pete's devilish bunkers.

"So, what kind of car do you drive?" Bill asked.

"What kind of car do I drive?"

He shrugged. "I figured I'd better ask so I can justify your greens fee on an expense report."

"I drive a three series BMW."

"Good car."

"I'm looking at trucks right now, thinking about the Toyota Tundra."

"Buy it."

"Yeah?"

He nodded as another explosion of sand, but no ball, flew up from the bunker. "When we were retooling the F-150 we tore down the Tundra and tried to reverse engineer it. It's a great truck. And if you tell anybody I told you this, I'll find you and kill you in your sleep."

After Stan finally threw the ball out of the bunker and we finished putting, we got back in our carts and rode toward the four-hole infield loop. The track had been hot for about twenty minutes, which meant that cars were running when we passed through the infield tunnel. It sounded like we were trapped in the engine of a 747.

"So much for a quiet round," I said.

"That's not why you play here," Bill said.

Stan chimed in with, "Why exactly did we play here?"

"You're not having fun?"

"Oh yeah—boatloads. I don't know Pete Dye, but I think he should be made to play out here, and we should beat him with a stick until he breaks eighty."

"Pete's eighty years old," I said.

"Good, then he won't be able to run very fast."

When we got to the seventh tee, we could barely hear ourselves yell. Eddie Cheever, the 1998 Indy 500 winner and a darn good golfer, was flying through the short chute between Turns One and Two. I got out of the cart and tried to focus on the par three ahead. As Eddie took a high line through Turn Two, I pulled a six-iron out of the bag. The hole was 193 yards with a slight tailwind. Sam Hornish was right behind Cheever. As the cars exited Turn Two, they screamed straight toward us.

There is no sound in the world like the 10,000-rpm howl of an Indy car. It's even more intimidating when you're standing on a tee box a few feet from the track with the cars coming at your back—a tough enough shot without the distraction. The elevated tee gives you a great view of the entire track, but the green is also elevated, reminiscent of the Redan or "fortress" holes of Scotland. Anything missed left or right will bounce and run away from the green, leaving a tough uphill pitch.

From the moment I teed up my ball I started telling myself, "They're not going to hit you. Yes, they sound like they're about to run over you, but there's thirty feet of asphalt and a big chain-link fence between you and two-hundred-mile-an-hour death. Tune them out. They're not going to hit you." Then as I addressed the shot, I heard a driver get into the throttle exiting Turn Two, about two hundred yards behind me on a direct line to my right butt cheek.

I backed away. "They're not going to hit you. Relax. It's just noise," I said to myself.

Looking to the exit of Turn One I saw Helio Castroneves swing to the inside through the short chute, and take it high toward the outside wall in Turn Two.

"Easy now, go through your normal routine."

Eeeeeeeehhhh-owwwwwwww.

"See, he didn't hit you. Take your time. Make a good swing."

It took four tries and Bill saying, "Track's going to be hot for another hour; you can't wait 'em out," before I finally made a swing. Thankfully, I hit a thin cut that landed in the front fringe and scooted back to the center of the green.

If Stan let the cars bother him, it didn't show. He would have topped it in the water on a calm, quiet day too.

"Blame it on the noise," I said.

Bill missed the green as well, but advanced it pin high on the left. After he hit, we all stood on the tee and watched another group of cars scream through Turn Two and fly by us on the back stretch.

"Is this one of the strangest things you've ever done in golf?" Bill asked.

I thought about all the stuff I'd been fortunate enough to do in the game: the places I'd played and the people I'd met; the time I took a leak next to Prince Andrew in the clubhouse at Royal Lytham and St. Annes and the potty joke I made about shaking hands with royalty; the potty joke President George H. W. Bush told me as we were watching the Presidents Cup together; and the joke-a-minute round I played with David Feherty. Then I looked at the track again as Scott Sharp got up to speed for his first hot lap of the day and whizzed by us so fast it was hard for my vision to follow.

"No, you guys aren't half bad," I said. "I've played with crappy golfers all my life."

EIGHT

Rolling Down the Fairway
with a Rock Star

(or "Hit the Ball, Alice!")

Golf is like a character X-ray machine. If you want to know if someone is a good person or a kick-him-to-the-curb jackass, spend four uninterrupted hours together on the golf course. In that time, you'll get a glimpse at how the person handles adversity, embarrassment, success, failure, pressure, anger, joy, unfairness, and guilt. Want to know if your CFO buddy is embezzling funds? Look at the drops he takes and how creative he gets with his scorekeeping. Interested in knowing if your lawyer is a ruthless SOB? See if he screws you on the course.

You will also be a party to some of life's more fascinating conversations. For example, sitting on the seventeenth tee at the TPC at Sawgrass, the devilish island par three, I answered the ringing cell phone of my instructor Cindy Reid as she was lining up the most intimidating nine-iron shot in golf.

"Cindy Reid's phone," I said.

"Well, who the f*** is this? And where the f*** is Cindy Reid?"

"Nobody, and she's hitting her tee shot right now," I said. "May I tell her who's calling?"

"This is Charles Barkley. Tell her I got to get some help. I can't hit it worth a shit. She's got to save me before I kill somebody."

Not the kind of thing you hear every day. Nor are you likely to hear a former president talk about death and urination. During one of his speed golf rounds at Cape Arundel in Kennebunkport, Maine, former President Bush was forced to wait on the group ahead of him on a tee box that backed up to a graveyard. "When I die, I don't want to be buried there," he said. When asked the logical follow-up question "Why?" the octogenarian ex-president said, "When my friends had to wait on this tee, they'd walk over there and piss on my grave."

And then there was the case of one of my partners in a golf event in Orlando who started one conversational thread with: "Bono is the Antichrist!"

This wasn't the sort of proclamation I expected, especially after he sank a twelve-footer for birdie on an all-you-want over-water bring-your-A-game-or-a-bucket-of-balls par three. No histrionics after the putt fell, no fist pumps, raised putters, or shouts of "Yeah" or "You da man." It was just another birdie from a player accustomed to making a boatload. He stopped talking just long enough to sink the putt, and then jumped back into his diatribe.

"I like U2," I said.

"Oh, I like them, too," he said, waving his hands in big swooping swirls as if to shoo away the swarm of thoughts to the contrary.

"But Bono"—he held up his fingers as he ticked off his list—"let's see, he's wealthy, he's worshipped all over the planet, he preaches world peace, and he wants to consolidate all religions. Who does that describe?"

In unison, I and the other members of our group said, "The Antichrist."

He threw his arms wide and walked away like Clarence Darrow at the end of a closing argument. "I rest my case."

"Ever tell him that to his face?" I asked.

"Absolutely," he said. "I've got a classic-rock radio program where I stick it to all the guys I've known for years. I had Tommy Shaw from Styx on a few weeks ago and accused him of writing the gayest song in rock history. 'Come Sail Away'? What, was that for all their sailor-suit-wearing fans?"

"What did he say?"

"He had a great comeback. He said, 'Look who's talking. At least I didn't write "Only Women Bleed." ' "

The fact that my playing partner had written that ballad sparked an ancient memory. I said, "When I bought that forty-five my parents thought *you* were the Antichrist."

That sparked another good-natured laugh, one of many I shared during my round with Vincent Damon Furnier, an Arizona resident who, for the last thirty-five years, has gone by the name Alice Cooper, a gender-bending moniker that Vince first claimed was the name of a witch who visited him during a Ouija board session. Later Alice (Vince legally changed his name in 1974) admitted that he came up with the name as he was daydreaming about a little pigtailed school girl hiding a hatchet behind her back.

Vince (Alice) and his merry band of cross-dressing shock-rockers first called themselves "The Spiders," but bug names were becoming passé. Then they changed it to "The Nazz," a name they figured was safe and obscure enough. Then (go figure) they found out Todd Rundgren also had a band called "The Nazz." Out of frustration, Vince hit paydirt when he decided to dress as an androgynous witch and go by the name "Alice Cooper."

He's the most infamous shock-rock musician in history—in fact, he was the very guy who spawned the term "shock rock." At the height of his popularity in the seventies, Alice's live show featured rock-related infant executions, complete with lullaby dolls and fake blood. He used guillotines and electric chairs as props as he pranced around stage in witch makeup with a boa constrictor around his neck. Now, as we strolled from the seventh green to the eighth tee at ChampionsGate in Orlando, he was calling Bono, whose only crime against humanity was the Zooropa tour, the Antichrist.

"Man, I love this driver," Alice said as he pulled out Callaway's newest big-headed titanium. "I think I'm going eighteen more after lunch."

The man whose first hit was titled "Eighteen" stood three weeks shy of fifty-eight years old that morning. And he was living *la vida grande,* playing golf by day and rocking to sold-out clubs by night when he wasn't sitting in his Phoenix studio broadcasting *Nights with Alice Cooper,* his syndicated nine-to-midnight radio show that went out to a hundred stations five nights a week. After forty years in a business where most people are lucky to make it five,

Alice had evolved into a combination golf freak and rock star, a man living a fantasy life.

"How many rounds a year do you play?" I asked.

"Do two rounds a day count?"

"That many?"

"If it's not raining, I'm playing."

"Doesn't rain much in Phoenix, does it?"

The big grin spread on his face again. "Not much," he said.

With his ponytail strategically tucked beneath his USS *George Washington* cap—"I'm doing a huge USO tour this summer, whatever I can do to help those guys"—he looked like a typical Florida golf nut, a middle-aged, middle-handicapper. His infectious, cat-in-the-hat smile said it all: He got the joke, even if the rest of us didn't.

Callaway Golf had set up the outing, another media freebee at one of central Florida's many golf factories. The centerpiece of ChampionsGate's 36-hole complex was the Omni Hotel, which stuck out on the barren I-4 sandscape, a symbol of everything native Floridians had grown to despise about their state. An area that was orange groves and interstate just a few years before had transformed into another golf-and-go resort, one which boasted on its website that it was "Just 15 minutes from Walt Disney World Resorts and Universal Studios."

Before teeing off that morning I'd thumbed through some marketing materials. "Oh, look," I said to a fellow writer at the breakfast table, "it says here they're known for their 'first-class amenities including valet parking, iced towel service, and digital

GPS Prolink, Caddy System, the number one GPS system,' which it says 'acts as a professional caddie to improve your skills, experience PGA-type scoring, and enhance your overall play.'"

"Does it blow you at the turn?" my mealmate said.

"Doesn't say, but let me know if you find out."

The festivities were to be grand with or without the bells and whistles. Alice, one of Callaway's star promoters, was there to play golf and glad-hand, and Annika Sorenstam was scheduled to troll the fairways playing one hole with every group. Not only did I talk my way into the event—which included breakfast, lunch, eighteen holes, two dozen new golf balls, and a sneak peak at Callaway's newest line of woods and irons—I got the premier pairing with *No More Mr. Nice Guy* himself.

"How much are you playing while you're here?" I asked Alice as the golf cart rolled up the fairway.

"If the weather holds, I'll get in eighteen more this afternoon. We're doing a show at the House of Blues tomorrow night, but I think I've got time to get in a round in the morning."

"So, thirty-six today, and eighteen tomorrow?" I said.

"Unless I get out early enough tomorrow to get in twenty-seven."

My view of Alice thereby skyrocketed, even before he started sinking birdie putts left and right. On the par-five eighth, he ripped a drive down the middle, did an on-camera interview for The Golf Channel, striped a three-wood to the front of the green, signed a couple of autographs, hit a bump-and-run seven-iron chip to three feet, plugged Callaway for a local newscast, and sank the putt for birdie.

"I want your life," I said.

He grinned and said, "I know."

The disconnect I was having between the man who screams *"School's been blown to pieces"* and the tanned AARP guy in FootJoys grew with each fairway Alice hit.

"This driver's the real deal," he said, another shameless plug he delivered without a hint of guilt or hesitation.

"Yeah, yeah, yeah," I said. "But did you really bite the head off a chicken?"

"Let me tell you what happened," he said. "We were a young group, just cut our first record with Frank Zappa's label, and we were touring like crazy. So, it's September of sixty-nine and we're playing the Toronto Rock 'n' Roll Revival. Middle of the show somebody throws a chicken on the stage. I didn't know livestock. So I grab this chicken and figure, hey, it's a bird; it has wings; it should be able to fly. I throw it out into the crowd. The thing flutters in the air for a second and then falls into the crowd."

"And got ripped to shreds."

"So they say."

"No head biting, huh?"

"Frank [Zappa] called me and said, 'Did you bite the head off a chicken and drink its blood on stage?' I said, 'What are you nuts?' And Frank says, 'Well, whatever you do, don't tell anybody you didn't do it.' "

Halfway through the round, I got a nickname. "You're a stick, Stevie," Alice said, after I'd hit a fairway bunker shot to within four feet, a good ten feet closer than anyone else in the group. "That's a Rock Hudson."

"What's a Rock Hudson?" I asked.

"One that's inside the boys."

He was full of them. A Sharon Stone was a shot that "looks better from a hundred yards out"; a Rush Limbaugh was one that's "fat and right"; a Thurman Munson was "a dead yank"; and an Angelina Jolie putt was one that "looks straight, but veers off to the left at the end."

Alice recorded twenty-nine albums in thirty-six years, including collaborations with Zappa, Bon Jovi, and Aerosmith. He also claimed to play two hundred rounds of golf a year, including appearances on the hit-and-giggle celebrity pro-am circuit. And he couldn't have been a greater partner. As we stood on one of the tees, he was in the middle of a story about being out carousing with Ozzie and Bowie. I said, "You seem to have made it out the other side a lot better than those guys."

"Bowie's doing great," he said. "Ozzie . . . not so much."

"He won't be playing thirty-six anytime soon."

Just then, Annika rolled up to the tee. "Hey, guys. Hi, Alice," she said. That greeting seemed wrong on many levels.

Annika missed the fairway and made par when she played with us. Then after a "Great to see you, Alice," and a "Good to see you, too, Annika," she was off.

On the next tee, Alice pulled one of the parlor tricks most of his fans had never seen. He took a tee out of his pocket and threw it into the ground like throwing a switchblade into a stump. Then he bent over and placed the ball on the perfectly balanced tee.

"No way," I said. "Can you do it again?"

He did.

"Want to see it again?" he said. And he produced.

"That's something you don't see every day," I said.

"Want to bet I can do it again?"

"No thanks. I get the picture."

He threw another tee in the turf, sticking it perfectly upright, and said: "So, I'm doing this with Rocco [Mediate] and [Phil] Mickelson in Palm Springs. Mickelson will bet on anything. So he says, 'Five hundred says you can't do it again.' So, I do it again. He says, 'Double or nothing.' And I do it again. He kept upping the bet, and I kept sticking them in the ground. I set a personal record of thirty-eight in a row."

"How much did Mickelson lose?"

He grinned. "Where do we think you have to hit it on this hole?"

I took that to mean it was a staggering sum.

On the sixteenth tee, I finally got an opportunity to use the line I'd waited for all day. He'd just thrown another tee like a dart into the closely mown Bermuda grass when one of the salesmen from Callaway rode up in a cart, shook his hand, and asked his opinion on the best backbeat drummer of all time. "John Bonham or Charlie Watts?" the guy asked.

"Watts is great," he said. "But Bonham was something special."

They went on like this for another ninety seconds. That was when I saw my opening. "Hey," I yelled, "hit the ball, Alice."

"You know, I've never heard that one before," he said. " 'Hit the ball, Alice,' 'Nice putt, Alice,' and my all-time favorite, 'We're not worthy.' I get 'em every time. Of course when I win, you can call me 'Your Majesty.' "

The "we're not worthy" line threw me for a second, and then it hit me: Alice played himself in *Wayne's World*. In one scene Alice, in full makeup, explained the Native American origins of the name Milwaukee, or some such thing. Dana Carvey and Mike Myers as Garth and Wayne bowed down when they met Alice, and chanted "We're not worthy!"

I cursed myself for not remembering it sooner, and then cursed myself for remembering it at all. Another hundred synapses wasted.

"Yeah, it's funny: I'm remembered more for that movie than anything else. I coach Little League baseball," he said, invoking more disconnected mental imagery. "So, I'm at the plate hitting grounders, trying to teach the kids to field the ball and make a throw. They're not paying any attention at all. The ball's going through their legs, and rolling by them. They're staring at me. Finally, I called them in and said, 'Guys, what's wrong? Nobody's paying attention.' The first baseman looks at me and says, 'Coach Cooper, how did you get on *Wayne's World*?"

Fifteen minutes later, Coach Cooper rolled in a curling twelve-footer for another birdie on the final hole of our round, but not his final hole of the day. "Enjoyed it, guys," he said. "Looks like I got time for at least another nine if not more."

"We're not worthy," I said.

"Good one."

Only I meant every word.

NINE

Walking Through a
Winter Golfing Land

(or You Mean You Intended to Play Golf in the Snow?)

Some jaunts in the name of journalism are so outrageous they embarrass even the most seasoned freeloader. A first-class romp through the Swiss Alps playing snow golf with Ryder Cup captain Sam Torrance and supermodel Jodie Kidd qualifies as one of those.

The term "snow golf" itself would normally be enough to give me pause. Playing golf in the snow had always been one of those accidents I'd been embarrassed to confess—the forecast called for mid-forties and sunny, but flurries started on the seventh tee, that sort of thing. There were the few occasions when I played on a warm afternoon before all the snow melted from the shadows after a winter storm, but that didn't count. Never would I have considered flying across an ocean for the express purpose of playing in the white stuff. This was until I got a call from the director of marketing for Chivas Regal asking me to participate in the Chivas Snow Golf Championship in St. Moritz.

"Snow golf?" I said, assuming I had heard wrong.

"It's the twenty-sixth annual playing of the Chivas Snow Golf Championship," he said. "Part of the 'Chivas Life' series. We also have elephant polo in Thailand."

"I'm not your guy for polo."

"We would love to have you for snow golf. A good number of professionals are coming. Jodie Kidd will be defending her women's title."

Not being up to speed on the supermodel front I Googled Ms. Kidd. The first image to pop up was a leggy blonde on the roof of a Maserati wearing nothing but Jimmy Choo stilettos and a Bogart fedora.

"I'm in," I said.

Two weeks later, at a time when sports like downhill skiing and curling dominated Swiss weekends, I and eighty other nitwits from as far away as Korea, Beijing, Moscow, and San Juan, Puerto Rico, flew into Zurich and took a train through the mountains to the lovely village of St. Moritz, where we were to play golf on a course that the head of the St. Moritz tourist board had designed and carved out of the snow.

The course was relatively flat, sitting on what, in the summer, was a pasture at the base of the main ski mountain in town. The first tee, marked by two ankle-high mounds of snow with Chivas signs sticking out, sat next to a curling court and a few yards away from the local outdoor hockey rink.

In my pre-tournament practice round, I learned that the rules of snow golf weren't much different from those of many Saturday afternoon dogfights played on courses from Shreveport to Savannah. We wore thermals, ski pants, a turtleneck, and boots, the same things you would wear if you were playing golf in February at home, and we improved our lies in the fairways, which were shaped and graded with the same plow used to groom nearby ski slopes. The only difference was that improving your lie in snow entailed putting your orange ball on a special tee, a one-inch rubber nub. You could even chip off a tee, which required a deft touch given that the frozen greens, which (honest to god, I'm not making this up) locals call "whites," are pocked with size-nine footprints.

"Is this course here throughout the winter, or was it made just for this event?" I asked an Austrian woman who came up behind me on the first tee.

"They play all winter here," she said. "Only one open championship, though."

"Are you playing in the tournament?"

"Of course: That's why we're here."

A witty comeback seemed inappropriate, since I was there for the same reason. At least the woman didn't fly nine hours and get her passport stamped to tromp around in the snow with a golf bag slung over her shoulder.

Another local rule stated that once your ball was on the whites, you could smooth the line of your putt with a greenside smoother, a four-by-four nailed to the end of a broomstick. This makeshift plow had the dual effect of knocking excess powder off your line and turning the whites into something akin to skating rinks. More than once, the members of my group, yours truly included, played slip-and-slide before going down in a bruising and embarrassing thud.

At least the supermodel remained upright, or so she claimed after the practice round.

"It's great fun, isn't it?" Jodie Kidd said in the clubhouse as she warmed her hands on a hot cup of cocoa. "Quite a bit different than your standard round, although you still have to hit the shots. I find it's a lot like links golf. You have to hit a lot of bumping shots that skid along the ground, and you're going to have some odd bounces."

Few things in life are more surreal than getting snow golf tips from a supermodel. I had to disagree with her strategy, though.

"I found that I need to keep it in the air, because you never know what kind of skids and bounces you're going to get," I said.

Jodie cocked her head and said, "Really? I find that the ball scoots on the ice regardless of how it comes in, so it's easier for me to hit the knockdown shots that would normally run."

"That works fine until the ball falls into a huge footprint." Then I said, "Jodie, you realize we're debating the best way to play golf in the snow."

She shrugged. "It's still golf," she said.

Just when I thought things couldn't get stranger, I found myself sitting in a hotel bar with European Ryder Cup captain Sam Torrance at three in the morning on the night of his wife's birthday.

"Stevie, you can't leave now," Sam said as he ordered his second liter of Chivas, putting him in a category all by himself.

"Sam, it's Suzanne's birthday," I said in my best please-let-me-save-you-from-yourself tone. Suzanne Torrance, a beautiful and charming former stage and television actress in the UK and the mother of three daughters, was standing five feet away looking none too pleased, but not at all surprised.

"And it's our anniversary," Sam said, raising a finger and an eyebrow as if he'd just remembered. "I married her on her birthday, surprised her with it, really. I planned the whole wedding and told everyone except her. Finally, I handed her a ring and said, 'Let's get married right now.' She said yes, but didn't realize I meant right that minute."

"And look what it's gotten me," Susanne piped up through a tight smile.

"Aye, you're still a catch," Sam said.

"I'm going to bed, Sam," I said. "You'll have to tackle me to stop me, which means you'll have to get off that stool."

"You should stay."

"Happy birthday, Suzanne."

"I hope so," she said, although her tone didn't sound promising.

I made three consecutive birdies followed by three straight bogeys to finish sixth in the Chivas Snow Golf Championship, tying me with Spanish touring pro Gonzalo Fernández-Castaño. I also waxed European Tour stalwarts Paul Eales and Henrik Bergqvist.

Jodie failed to successfully defend in the women's division, finishing five shots behind Swiss pro and former University of South Carolina Gamecock Caroline Ruminger.

"I just haven't played enough to stay competitive," Jodie said. "Between the car racing [she drives in the Maranello Racing Circuit for Team Maserati] and launching my own shoe line, I just haven't had the time."

"Jodie, it's snow golf," I said.

She set her jaw, and said, "Still."

To the surprise of absolutely no one, Sam was unable to compete, citing a sudden outbreak of tendonitis as the culprit.

He did, however, raise a toast to all of us afterward as the whiskey flowed on the deck overlooking the curling court.

"All good fun, eh?" Sam said as he tipped his glass. "We'll have to do it again sometime."

Part Three

Golf with the Champions

(or Why Are You Playing with Me?)

TEN

The Asian Invasion

(or How I Sort of Beat a British Open Champion)

In case you failed to notice, the LPGA Tour has a few Asian players. And, again in case you missed it, they're pretty darn good.

In less than a decade, South Korea has become a farm league for the women's tour, a phenomenon akin to Kenya's distance-running dominance. There are more than thirty South Korean women playing the top level, up from two in 1998 when one of the pair, twenty-year-old Se Ri Pak, won the U.S. Women's Open and the LPGA Championship in her rookie year. By 2002, the most common surnames on the LPGA were Kim, Lee, and Park, and the leaderboards each week were filled with first names like Mi Hyun, Kyeong, Ha Na, Hee-Won, Seo-Yeon, Joo Mi, and Na Ri. Today a country the size of Indiana has more women players on the tour than any country other than our own. And in 2006, Korean players won a third of the events and half the prize money on the LPGA Tour.

A fair number of the game's "traditionalists" didn't handle it well. Australian Jan Stephenson, one of the glam girls of the LPGA in the 1970s whose biggest—*ahem*—exposure came when she posed nude in a bathtub full of golf balls, said, "Asians are killing our tour. Absolutely killing it." Lest you think I've taken those comments out of context, the then fifty-one-year-old Stephenson, who is the poster girl for extreme makeovers gone bad, and is today one facelift away from bursting like the *Hindenburg*, went on to say, "Their lack of emotion, their refusal to speak English when they can speak English: They rarely speak. We have two-day pro-ams where people are paying a lot of money to play with us, and they say 'hello' and 'goodbye.' Our tour is predominately international and the majority of them are Asian. They've taken it over. . . . And all those Negroes are ruining the NFL, too."

Okay, I made that last line up. But the rest of this came out of the mouth of a player with sixteen LPGA victories, including three major championships. In response, the commissioner of the LPGA called Stephenson "an ambassador" of the woman's game.

No one knows how many Korean golfers have studied eighteenth-century French literature, but the Asians on the LPGA took to heart Pierre Ambroise François Choderlos de LaClos's quip about revenge being a dish best served cold. Today, the biggest single income generator for the LPGA Tour is its Korean television contract.

The curious explorer in me wanted to know more about this sudden golfing migration from North Asia. I also wanted to know how, exactly, South Korea came to dominate the money list, and raise the ire of many a participant on the American LPGA Tour.

So while I was in Orlando I ventured up the street from ChampionsGate to another golf-and-condo cluster-club called Reunion, the home of the LPGA's Ginn Resorts Championship. My playing partner for the day was Jeong Jang, the leading money winner among the Koreans that year, and the winner of the 2005 Women's British Open.

Far from being one of Jan Stephenson's "hello" and "good-bye" girls, J.J. was an engaging and funny fireplug of a girl (the LPGA media guide listed her at five foot two, but she had to stand straight to reach the five-foot mark). What she lacked in height she made up for in spunk and personality. When I struck up a conversation with her at a cocktail party once, she not only admitted that she didn't understand everything I said, but, as she put it, "My English probably better than your Korean."

Of that there was no doubt.

Three months after that chance meeting, I saw J.J. wheel into the parking lot at Reunion in a Z3 BMW with the top down and the radio blasting Kanye West. It hadn't taken long for this Asian flower to adapt. A couple of things were still very Korean, though. "We got couple joining us," J.J. said after greeting me. On cue, two Korean men got out of another car and walked over. "This Andy Hwang," J.J. said. "He work with The Golf Channel."

"I'm here to translate if there's a point where you get stuck, or if you need something explained in a little more detail," Andy said in born-and-raised-in-California English.

This was a ruse, of course, one I recognized immediately. Single Korean women in their twenties did not ride off in golf carts with strange American men. Asian decorum required a chaperone, and an excuse. Andy provided both.

"This is Junsik Lee," Andy said, introducing the second guy in the group.

"He play in Korea and is here taking lessons with my coach," J.J. quickly added, another tidbit that didn't ring exactly true. I later learned that while Junsik did, indeed, play in Korea, and was, as advertised, taking lessons from J.J.'s coach, he was also her boyfriend, something that didn't get broadcast to strangers either.

Poor Junsik spoke no English beyond "good shot."

"He'll be my partner," I said to J.J. as I pointed a thumb at Junsik. "We'll play you and Andy for a beer."

She flashed a grin the size of Texas, and said, "You're on."

As is the case with any first-time round with new acquaintances, it took a couple of holes for everyone to fall into a rhythm. This was doubly true for Junsik, but that was probably my fault. On the second green, I walked by, patted him on the butt, and said, "Knock it in, partner." He jumped a foot and gave me a "Thanks for offering, but I'm not into that" look of panic.

I turned to J.J. and said, "How do you say, 'Knock it in, partner' in Korean?"

She laughed. "You don't." Then she said something to Junsik in their native tongue.

He gave a sigh of relief, and made the putt to keep us even through two.

On the next tee we caught the group ahead of us, so I asked J.J. how she got into golf. The English wasn't perfect, but the story sure was. She is the youngest and, by far, most gregarious of three daughters of Kyoung Suk Lee and Suk Jung Jang. Her father, Suk Jung, a retired police detective in Daejeon, took up golf after rotator cuff surgery and one too many birthdays eliminated his days on the baseball diamond. Her mother, a striking but demure woman who could have been a model, had to get her spark plug youngest daughter out of the house before young Jeong drove the whole family nuts. So Mom shooed J.J. to the golf course to fetch Suk Jung for dinner. Once there, J.J. watched her father and decided, "This ain't so tough."

Suk Jung watched his daughter hit balls and saw something special. "He not like other Korean dads," J.J. said. "He say, 'If you want to do this, you need to be dedicated,' but he not push. I want to play, so he there with me."

I knew what she meant by "not like other Korean dads." I had seen it in the junior and amateur ranks, and even, to some extent, on tour. Fathers of daughters are shown a huge level of deference in Korean culture. Overbearing elders are treated like the blind masters in bad kung fu movies: head down, bow, "Thank you, sir, may I have another." Dad doesn't like something in your golf swing? You hit balls until your hands bleed while he berates every shot. Pops doesn't think you're making enough five-footers? You stand on the putting green until you make a hundred in a row even if it means he has to pull the car around to shine headlights on the hole. Win a tournament, Father Dearest gets the credit. And that's for the twelve-year-olds.

The result has been a huge influx of great Korean female golfers. Boys, you see, are encouraged to stay in school to become doctors, lawyers, or other noble professionals. Girls hang out with dad and learn to shoot in the sixties.

Once the girls get on tour the problems really start. Se Ri Pak had a terrible time with her dad, who insisted on being Big Man on Campus well after she became a major champion and future Hall of Famer. After a while, Se Ri threw up her hands and went through one of the most spectacular slumps in golf, a period where she hated the game. It wasn't until she forced her father offstage that she rebounded. Other players tell similar stories. One Korean pro actually slept in her car before the final round of a tournament she was leading, because her father didn't think she was putting well enough to win.

"So, how often did your dad watch you play?" I asked J.J.

She looked at me like I had spinach hanging out of my nose. "Every day," she said with a "What do you mean?" shrug.

"Your father was with you every day?"

"Sure. He didn't make me go to the golf course. I want to do that. But once I say what I want, he go every day."

"For how long?"

"All day."

"No, I mean, how many weeks did he do that?"

"Seven year."

"Seven years!"

"Yeah, why?"

"Your father was with you on the golf course every day for seven years?"

"More, really," she said. "He was with me in Korea every day for seven year. Then I qualify for the tour, and he move here with me."

I had done a little homework before our round, so I knew that J.J. had been the top-ranked amateur in Korea after she won the 1997 Korea Women's Open and the 1998 Korea Women's Amateur. Both those years she had played on the Korea Women's National Team, where she finished fourth individually in the World Team Amateur Championship, the most prestigious amateur team event in the world outside the Walker and Curtis cups.

"So, did you always know you wanted to come here and play the tour?"

"No!" she shouted and waved her arms. "I figure I become a school teacher. I go to school and study kinesiology, and physical education, and figure, that's it: I will teach and coach."

"What changed your mind?"

"My dad took me to see Alison Nicholas the summer she win the U.S. Women's Open. She came to Korea for an exhibition. When I see her, my dad say, 'She is not much taller than you.' I say, 'Not much taller! She shorter than me!' That's when I realize I can try this."

J.J. qualified for the LPGA on her first attempt in 1999, and has been one of the top performers ever since.

"Your dad moved here with you after you qualified?"

"Yeah, I didn't drive then, so he came here and drive and take care of things. Neither of us speak English, so it was very hard. We couldn't make hotel reservations or order a meal. We drive to the tournament, show up at the hotel, and I hand them a credit card and smile." She demonstrated the big innocent smile that had to have earned her a few chortles from hotel desk clerks. "If they say something I get the phone and call a Korean friend who speak English and hand them the phone."

"That had to be rough," I said. "I mean, it's easier for an American to go to Asia, where you can always find somebody who speaks English. Not too many hotel clerks and pizza delivery men speak Korean."

"You got that right," she said, proving that her American phraseology was improving each year. "And it not just speaking. My dad couldn't read road signs. One time we turn down one-way street the wrong way. Big sign says 'Do Not Enter,' but it might as well say 'Eat at Joe's.' Then I see this big truck coming at us, and scream 'Dad!' He say, 'What?'"

After I recovered from the laughter, I said, "You know if this golf thing doesn't work out, you've a future in comedy."

She grinned and said, "I know."

In a stunning turn of events, I rolled in two birdies on the front side and Junsik made two more. We made the turn two up on J.J. and Andy, which didn't sit well with my cart companion. Starting at the tenth, she made three birdies in a row while her partner played condo-tag with a sleeve of Pro V1s. I scrapped in one more birdie on the eleventh, which kept the match all square with six to play.

"What made you choose to live in Orlando?" I asked, assuming I would get the standard "taxes, weather, and the airport" answer that made central Florida a haven for athletes from all sports.

"We start out in San Francisco," she said. "It's great. I love it, but I realize I could live there and never learn English. So I say to my dad, 'No, if I'm going to play in America, I have to learn English.' I move here where I have no choice."

"Wow," I said. "You moved to Florida speaking no English?"

"I could say 'good shot.' My English still not great, but sometimes people don't try to listen. Like I trying to order ice cream the other day, and the guy say, 'What flavor?' and I say, 'Vanilla.' He cock his head and say, 'What?' So I say, 'Come on, even if I speaking Swahili, how many flavors you got that start with V?' "

Ten minutes later I rolled in my fourth birdie putt of the day, and Junsik made a great par to halve the next hole, which prompted me to dance across the green, high-five my partner, and give him my best "You da man!"

That he understood. "No," he said, "you da man!"

J.J. found no humor in our histrionics. We were one up with four to play, and she was bearing down.

"I can't believe he made that putt," she said. "He not that good."

"I'd tell him you said that if he spoke English."

"I know, that why I only say it to you."

"So, are you and Se Ri friends?" I asked as we waited on the next tee and watched storm clouds gather over Kissimmee.

"We are now," she said. "When I first come out, she older, so there was . . . separation."

Now it was my turn to cock my head. "What do you mean?" I asked.

"In Korea, someone who is older, even if it only one year, should be respected by anybody younger. So, when I first get here,

Se Ri can never speak to me first. I speak to her, and she answer, but she never walk up and say, 'Hey, J.J., how you doin'?'"

"Is it that way now?"

"Not with Se Ri. She great. But with others it's still that way, just Korean way."

"I don't know any Americans who know that about Korean culture."

She balled a fist and hit me in the arm. "You tell them," she shouted. "You a writer. That's why you here."

"No, I'm here to beat you out of a beer," I said.

"We'll see about that."

Junsik and I were one up standing in the middle of the seventeenth fairway. That's when heaven opened up and lightning flashed all around us. I grabbed my ball and hopped into the cart. J.J. barely stopped the E-Z Go to pick me up. We flew back to the clubhouse.

"I guess that means we won," I said.

"No way! We didn't finish."

"We didn't play any more holes than you did," I said. "Match ended at sixteen. We were one up. I'll take a Miller Lite."

"That not right."

"And life's not fair."

"You got to come back. That not right."

"I've never beaten a major champion before."

"You still haven't. That not right."

One week later, Jeong Jang shot 13 under par and won the Wegman's LPGA Championship in suburban Rochester by one shot over Julieta Granada. After the win, I sent her a note that said, "Losing that beer must have really pissed you off. Let me know when you need another motivator. I'll be happy to oblige."

The phone message I got back was short and to the point.

"Don't brag. That not right."

ELEVEN

An Afternoon with Arnie

(or There's a Reason He's the King)

And then one day I got one of the best phone calls a golfer could ever dream possible. It came from the 724 area code, a number I didn't recognize, but one I answered anyway. Good thing: The voice on the line said, "Oh, hi, Steve. This is Gina in Mr. Palmer's office. Mr. Palmer asked me to call you. He's got an opening for golf here in Latrobe next Tuesday, and was wondering if you could come up."

I cleared my throat and said, "You know, Gina, I think I'm free that day. Tell Mr. Palmer thank you. I'd love to play."

"Great. Meet him here at the office about eleven o'clock next Tuesday, and you can go over to the club together."

Mr. Palmer in Latrobe was Arnold Palmer, the King, the last living legend from the golden age of sports. For the first time in my life, I started getting nervous about a round a week before arriving at the course.

I first met Arnold Daniel Palmer during a rain delay at the Masters sometime in the early seventies, although in my case "met" was in the eye of the beholder. I was a hefty prepubescent kid with a bad haircut who walked past the Pinkertons and into the back entrance of the Augusta National clubhouse with a nod, a smile, and not a credential to my name, a prelude to a future career of sliding in where I didn't belong. That day Arnie, the Man at Augusta and everywhere else he played, was standing just inside the clubhouse, his left hip resting on the chair railing.

As I rushed in, his eyes caught mine. I stopped as if I'd been hit with a paralyzing ray gun. It was not a cold stare. Arnie always looked at you with a twinkle and a smile, like an old pal itching to catch up or an uncle about to tell you an off-color joke. Our encounter only lasted a few seconds. I introduced myself, and he said, "Nice to meet you." Then he looked at the "grounds only" ticket flapping on the front of my hard-collar Munsingwear shirt.

"You know, you shouldn't be in here with that," he said. "If they see you, they might ask you to leave the golf course."

He put his arm around my shoulder and looked around as if he were about to help me escape from a bank heist. Once he determined that the coast was clear, he gently walked me to a door with an awning where I could stand out of the rain without violating the terms of my patron pass.

"You okay, here?" Arnold asked, not sure if he should leave me without my parents.

"Yes, sir," I said in a voice with more cracks than a month-old

pound cake. Then it dawned on me that a once-in-a-lifetime op-
portunity was about to pat me on the back and walk away. "Wait,"
I said as I fumbled for the pairings sheet in my back pocket.
"May . . . may I get your autograph."

"Of course," he said as he took the damp sheet.

I was once again mesmerized. Anybody could have said "of
course," and left you with the impression that you were a bother.
Arnie made it sound like he was saying, "Gosh, I'm sorry. Of
course you can have an autograph. I should have thought of that."

It was a trait I would see countless times over the next thirty
years.

Like most reporters who had the privilege of covering the
King, I had sat through Palmer press conferences where I thought,
"This is the greatest athlete, ever." Then I read the transcripts in a
vain search for a quote where none existed. He had said nothing,
but done so in a way that made every reporter in the room feel
like a buddy. Even reporters who collapsed into rambling verbal
palsies could count on Arnie to smile and interrupt at just the
right time to rescue a drowning pal.

It wasn't just reporters who felt captivated by Arnold. Guy Kinnings, who heads IMG's European golf division, used to take his
new tour-player clients to hear Arnie give speeches. When Kinnings related the story to me, he said, "After the speech was over I
would always ask, 'Did you like it?' They'd always say, 'Of course.
He was great. The best I've ever seen.' Then I'd ask them, 'Can
you summarize what he talked about?' And they never could.
They'd just walked out of the speech, and they had no idea what
the man had talked about. I said to them, 'Exactly! It's not what he

says, because he really doesn't say much of anything. It's how he says nothing that makes Arnold Palmer the King.' "

That day in the seventies when a kid met Arnie at the Masters, the King handed over my autographed pairings sheet, patted me on the back, and said, "Enjoy the tournament," nothing extraordinary, and nothing that countless pros hadn't said to fans thousands of times. But like the millions of people who have met him in his half-century career in the game, I walked away thinking I had developed a lifelong friendship with Arnold Palmer.

Such was his gift. I saw it at tournaments for years: fans stopping him to chat as if he were an old high school buddy when it was obvious Arnie couldn't have called their names on a bet. I saw it with high-powered business executives who became socially incompetent kids in his presence. I saw it the Tuesday before the Bay Hill Invitational when a developer who was about to pay Arnold seven figures to design and build a golf course walked around the clubhouse to meet the great man himself. Arnold came out of the cart barn like he was greeting a long-lost cousin, and said, "I'm sorry I can't shake your hand. I've been working on the brake shoes of these golf carts and I'm greasy." In fact, he was still holding golf cart parts in his hands.

A few minutes later I saw the developer walk away smiling. "Wow" was all I heard him say.

Thirty-three years after his last PGA Tour victory, and two generations removed from his last major title, there was still no more approachable superstar than Arnold. "Nobody will ever replace him," Mark Calcavecchia said, and he was right. Even though Jack Nicklaus and Tiger Woods have more major titles, neither has received the worldwide adulation of Palmer. Thousands of pros have made more money; Palmer's total career tour earnings wouldn't have gotten him into the top thirty on the 2006 money list. But no one has surpassed Arnold as golf's most endearing personality. He is Everyman, only with ninety-two victories, a Cessna Citation X (the fastest private jet in the world), partial ownership of Pebble Beach, four green jackets, and millions of adoring fans.

And I was playing golf with him next Tuesday.

The invitation didn't come out of the blue. I had been fortunate enough to help write two of Arnold's books, so I'd spent a fair amount of one-on-one time with him. Every time we met during both of those projects, Arnold spent the first fifteen minutes asking about my golf game, my family, and me. That's when it dawned on me that Guy Kinnings was wrong: It wasn't how he said what he said that made him the King; he was the best because, no matter who you were, Arnold Palmer had the innate ability to make you feel like the most important person in the room. How are you? How is your family? How are you playing? And never were those questions disingenuous; he really cared. That was why Arnold was the King.

He also genuinely liked the books I'd helped him write. I contacted Arnold's staff and asked if he would like to play—"Just whenever he has an opening"—but I didn't expect an answer. That was what made the call from Gina so great. It confirmed what I'd come to know about Arnold Palmer. He didn't write off my request any more than he would have ignored a kid asking for an autograph. It's not in his nature.

So I booked a flight to Pittsburgh, and hit the range. I had to get my game ready for a royal audience.

Prior to the trip I worried about everything. I looked up Latrobe Country Club online to get an idea of the kind of course I was about to play. I worried about the clubs and balls in my bag (everything I owned had Titleist or Cobra on it; Arnie was the spokesman-for-life for Callaway). I even worried about the clothes I would wear.

Worrying about the weather never occurred to me.

I got into Pittsburgh early Monday afternoon and made the one-hour drive to Latrobe in just over forty-five minutes. I whistled my way past the grim clapboard mill houses sticking out like boils on the knuckles of the craggy landscape, and hummed a happy tune as my rental car bounced through every pothole in Western PA. The hotel—the Mountain View Inn—didn't have any views at all that I could find, unless traffic on Route 30 or the Arnold Palmer Pavilion at the local hospital qualified. The bar and restaurant had the kind of early-seventies wagon-wheel-spindle design that looked bad when Nixon was around. Ancient cartoon prints of hoity-toity top hat–wearing men delivering punch lines that were probably knee-slappers a century ago adorned the dingy walls.

I cared not a wit about any of it. I was playing golf with Arnie. I could have stayed in a jail cell and been happy.

That was until I woke up Tuesday morning to the steady patter of rain on my windowsill, *rat-a-tat-tatting* like the laughter of demons. By the time my eggs arrived I thought I was going to be sick, not from the food, which was fine, but from the rhythmic drip of water torture. It wasn't a gully washer like the one we'd had in New York, but rain was rain. I figured I would show up at Arnold's office, and Gina would say, "Oh, hi, thanks for coming. Sorry about the weather. We'll let you know when he has another opening."

About 10:30, I plopped my wet bottom in the seat of Hertz's cheapest midsize and drove halfheartedly toward the offices of Arnold Palmer Enterprises. As if driving to meet the King weren't intimidating enough, the directions to his office didn't do much to relax you. First you turned out of the parking lot away from the aforementioned Arnold Palmer Pavilion, then you made a right at the Arnold Palmer Regional Airport, and a quick left onto Arnold Palmer Drive. A mile or so later you saw Arnold Palmer's Latrobe Country Club on your right, a place where you could go into the grill and order an Arnold Palmer (tea sweetened with lemonade). Since the television on the corner is almost always turned to The Golf Channel (cofounded by Arnold Palmer), there was a good chance you could see a rerun of the documentary *Arnold Palmer: Golf's Heart and Soul.* Then, if you were there at the right time of year, you could rest assured that the man his own self would stop by your table and ask if you were enjoying lunch.

Directly across Arnold Palmer Drive from the club entrance was a narrow driveway winding up a wooded hill. There was no sign or entry statement except for a gate that's never locked. And why should it be? The road doesn't appear to lead anywhere. If anything, it looks like a back entrance to Latrobe High School, which can be seen sitting atop the hill.

A hundred or so yards up the road I saw a large low-rise house on the right. This was the house Arnold and his wife Winnie bought when they first went out on tour in 1955, a small L-shaped ranch with a garage jutting out on one side. For fifty years it remained Arnold's primary residence, although he added on to it so many times it looked like an elementary school.

A few more yards up the hill sat another white structure with a concrete stoop and a multicolored umbrella above the door. It looked like one of the understated cottages lining the tenth fairway at Augusta National. This was Mr. Palmer's office.

I parked the car, cracked the door, and opened my umbrella before I noticed another large dwelling under construction a little farther up the hill. Looked like Arnie was going to have neighbors. I would ask him about it if I got the opportunity; it didn't appear as though I would have much else to do.

When I walked into the foyer, it was like stepping into an American history book. There were the major championship trophies on the mantel against the right-hand wall, and the photos of Arnie with presidents and dignitaries from the past fifty years. Then I saw the dog a split second before it cold-nosed my wet pants.

"Hey, buddy, what's your name?" I said: another in a long list of incredibly stupid utterances. It wasn't like it was going to answer me.

"That's Mulligan," I heard a familiar voice say from the corner office. "Come here, Mulligan." And the dog trotted off with his tail and tongue wagging for his master.

Arnold walked out to greet me with the same twinkling smile

he'd had thirty-five years earlier when I was a trespassing kid at Augusta. But that was not what caught my eye this time. What made my heart leap was the rain jacket and hat he carried.

"You ready for some golf?" he said.

"That's why I came . . . and to see you, of course."

"Great. Let's head over and have some lunch, and we'll get out. A couple of members are joining us." Then he pointed to the window and the peppering rain. "This should blow out of here in an hour."

Not only was he the King, he was a darned good weatherman. The clouds parted moments before we were to tee off. By then I was fully immersed in all things Palmer.

On our way out I had pointed to the house on the hill and asked about new neighbors. "No, that's my new house," Arnold said. "Got a new wife, and a new dog; I guess I needed a new house."

Winnie had died of cancer in November 1999. In January 2005, Arnold married Kit Gawthrop, an old family friend from Palm Springs who looked so much like Winnie that people from Callaway actually called her "Winnie 2.0." I don't think anybody outside the family ever told Arnie how spooky it was to have a second wife look so much like the first, but I had to believe that his daughters had said, "Dad, do you realize you're marrying the same woman again?"

Kit joined us for lunch, as did Arnold's younger brother Jerry, who managed Latrobe Country Club, and Donald "Doc" Giffin, Arnold's press secretary and confidant for forty years. During the meal I learned that Arnold was as surprised as anyone by the iced tea and lemonade drink becoming synonymous with his name. "I like it, but I had no idea it would take off like it has," he said. And I learned that Jack Nicklaus's father, Charlie, had always called Arnie by his middle name, Daniel. But most of the meal, Arnold wanted to know about me. He was particularly interested in my trip to China and how the country had changed since he was there in the mid-eighties.

When we finished, he picked up the tab and said, "Let me get you a locker and we'll get ready to go."

I wanted to say, "Please don't," but I knew it was useless. Taking care of guests was what he did. Nothing I could say would stop him.

Ten minutes later I met the other guys in our group. Dr. Jim Bryan, a dentist in Latrobe, was a ten-time club champion at Latrobe Country Club (by far the most in the club's eighty-year history), and Marty Newingham was an industry exec in the area. Both were part of Arnold's regular Latrobe game. "You'll be riding with Jimmy," Arnold said.

As I threw my clubs on Jim's cart I noticed that Arnold had his own custom golf cart and that he would be riding alone. Not that I minded: He was, after all, Arnold Palmer, and he did own the club. What I hadn't expected were the two golf bags, big honking Callaway staff bags with his name and multicolored umbrella logo plastered on the panels. Okay, again he was Arnold Palmer, and he could have six bags if he wanted. But the two he had were jammed full of clubs.

I slipped over and counted them, and then said to Jim, "He's got forty-four clubs in there. Is he going to play with all of those?"

"Oh yeah," Jim said. "He's taken some out. He normally plays with sixty."

The consummate tinkerer, Arnold had six Callaway drivers, two full sets of iron, eight sand wedges, and every fairway wood and hybrid the Carlsbad plant could send. I even saw a couple of Hogan hybrids (Callaway bought the Hogan Company in 2003).

"I can't believe he's got Hogan stuff in there," I said. Arnold's rift with Ben Hogan was well known. Hogan didn't think much of Arnold's swashbuckling style or hit-it-hard golf swing, nor was the Hawk much of a fan of the whole Arnie's Army thing. Hogan could play an entire round without speaking to a soul. Arnie, on the other hand, interacted with his gallery on every shot. Plus, Arnold found Hogan to be abrupt and rude, the latter being unacceptable in the Palmer family. As far as Arnie was concerned, it took no talent at all to be nice.

The biggest example of the difference between the men was the deal at Winged Foot Golf Club in New York. The board at Winged Foot always had a couple of legendary players as members. The memberships were gifts, which was no small thing given that Winged Foot was the club every honest golfer in the Northeast wanted to join. The membership read like a Who's Who of New York bigwigs, and anyone who played out there—even tour players—did so with a member in the group. In the early seventies the board gave a membership to Ben Hogan. For the next quarter century, he never used it; he didn't go to the club once.

When Hogan died in 1997, the board gave his membership to Arnold. The King showed up, unannounced, at Winged Foot a couple of times a year, hanging out at the caddy master's stand, greeting other members, and hooking up with anybody who needed a game. That, in a nutshell, was why Hogan and Palmer never saw eye to eye.

Arnold never spoke unkindly of Hogan, but he never went out of his way to compliment him either. The Callaway guys love to tell the story of showing up at Arnold's office with a sample dozen of their newest Hogan golf balls. The ball was so new that the package was unmarked. When the guys gave Arnold the box, he thanked them and asked what they were. "It's the new Hogan ball," one of them said.

Arnold opened his hands and dropped the box on the floor, where it broke open. Golf balls bounced and rolled around like the ping-pong ball gag on *Captain Kangaroo*. Then, with perfect comedic timing, Arnold said, "Woops . . . I dropped them."

Jokes aside, I was still a little surprised to see him carrying Hogans in his two-bag collection.

"Oh, that's not the best part," Jim said. "He's ground the name off the sole plates."

On the first tee Arnold got straight to the point. "I play these two guys for five bucks," he said. "You can get in this if you want, or not. Whatever makes you comfortable."

There are a few moments in your life when you know you are in the middle of something special. Seeing Michael Jordan play basketball *and* baseball was one of those; seeing Hank Aaron and Willie Mays play in the same game was another. Being there for Tiger's four straight major championship wins was memorable. But I wasn't a participant in any of those events.

This was a never-gonna-happen-again opportunity. Before anyone else could speak, I said to Arnold, "Why don't you and I play Jim and Marty. That way you don't have to play against them in one match and with them in another."

He nodded, obviously impressed with my flawless logic, or keen opportunism. I never asked which.

"That okay with you guys?"

No one objected, and I gave myself a silent fist pump for seizing the moment. Then I ripped a tee shot down the middle of the first fairway and heard my partner say, "Well, we're not going to lack for clubhead speed today."

If I'd ever doubted it in the past, I knew then that there was a God.

Everyone hit it in play off the first. And as we rode down the path, Arnold turned back to us and said, "Do you know if it's cart path only?"

"You own the golf course," Jim said.

His cart swerved into the fairway, and we followed close behind.

"It's fine out here," Arnie said, and he reached into his pocket for his cell phone. A second later he had his brother on the line. "Jerry, send word out that these fairways are dry enough. There's no need to restrict the carts."

Before we finished the hole a marshal rode down the cart path and yelled, "Gentlemen, it's no longer cart path only."

"Thank you," Arnold said with a wave.

Some moments were more memorable than others. On the seventh tee, after I had failed to convert a birdie putt on the par-five sixth, my partner turned to me and said, "I expect you to do better. We're down. That's not gonna cut it."

Oh dear merciful Jesus, Arnold Palmer had just told me to cowboy up and get my ass in gear. My eyes were the size of dinner plates as I said, "Yes, sir," and hit the next tee shot in the middle of the fairway.

It didn't help. Despite two birdies from my partner, who still hit his ball out there with men who hadn't been born when he won his last major, we lost the front nine one up.

Then things got interesting.

On the tenth, a 210-yard par-three, the group ahead waved us up.

"Wow, I didn't see those guys before," I said.

Jim smiled and said, "They were staying ahead of us until they saw Arnie. They slowed down to let us catch them so they can tell their buds they let Arnie play through today."

"Happen a lot?"

"Every time we play."

"How often do you play?"

Jim thought for a second and said, "At least two or three times a week when he's up here. A few weeks ago my wife said, 'You care more about playing golf with Arnold Palmer than you do about your practice.' I said, 'And your point is?'"

"I hope you don't ever take this for granted," I said. "This is about as special as it gets. And it won't last forever."

"Don't worry, I don't. If he calls at eight in the morning and says 'Let's play,' I tell my office manager to get on the phones and reschedule my day. I realize what I've got."

"We play a five-dollar close-up on this one," Arnold said to me as Marty teed up and took a practice swing on the tenth.

"Fine by me."

Marty missed the green left.

"One down," Arnold said.

Jim missed long and left.

"Wide open."

I hit a solid four-iron pin high twelve feet left of the hole.

Jim said, "That looks like a winner." Marty agreed.

Arnold looked at us like we'd just insulted his mother. "What am I, chopped liver?" he said.

Then I saw something I hadn't seen all day. Arnold stepped it up a notch. Everything from his pre-shot waggle to the way he stared down the pin had an added air of intensity. The swing might have looked the same, but there was no question that we had gotten his attention by counting him out. At that moment, I realized how this man had won ninety-two professional tournaments including seven majors. He was the nicest guy in the world, but when we ignited the competitor in him, he was like a lion stalking a wildebeest.

He hit it to six feet.

"Guy's got four green jackets and two claret jugs, but the most important thing in the world for him right then was beating me out of that five-dollar close-up," I said as Jim and I rode to the green.

"Moments like that are why I'm out here with him three times a week."

I made my twelve-footer for birdie to win the hole, and

Arnold, who went from king of the jungle to avuncular host faster than you could turn off a light switch, bought us all a drink at the halfway house. He was telling jokes by the time we got to the eleventh tee.

"Is he like this with everybody?" I asked Jim.

"What do you mean?"

"I mean every time I'm around him he's bending over backwards to make sure I'm happy."

"You're not special. He's like that with everyone and he's like that all the time. His biggest thrill in life is making other people happy. I tell everyone that for somebody who's hard of hearing, Arnold Palmer is the best listener I've ever met."

He was also still the hard charger who lost as many tournaments as he won by going for broke on every shot: a fact he illustrated when we got to the twelfth. On the tee I saw a creek running across the fairway at what appeared to be the landing area. "How far to carry the water, partner?" I asked.

"Well, there's a great story about that," Arnie said. "It's two hundred and forty-four yards to carry that water. And I used to tell everybody that if there ever came a day when I couldn't carry it, I'd know it was time to give up the game. I bet I haven't carried it three times this year, and I'm still out here."

My mind went into calculator mode: Two-forty-four into a cool damp wind meant I had to step on a driver to stay out of Arnold's quit-for-life qualifier. I hit first and put everything I had into a tee shot that cleared the water by a good six paces, just enough for me to say "whew" as my knees buckled.

Arnold then hit a great drive, one of his best of the day, which flew straight down the center of the fairway, and plopped with a splash in the middle of the creek. "Damn!" he said. Then he put his arm around me and said, "I guess I've got to quit."

Marty and Jim both hit it over, but not by much. As we rode down the cart path behind Arnold, Jim slapped my leg and said, "Bet you a buck he drops a ball on this side of the creek and gets up and down for par."

"I can't bet against my partner," I said.

"Okay, but remember I offered."

Thirty seconds later Arnold hit a nine-iron to within three feet of the hole where he made the putt for par.

"Told you," Jim said as we rode to the thirteenth. "He does it nine times out of ten. If he would hit three-wood off the tee and lay up short of the creek he'd make birdie every time. But he can't. No matter how practical it is to lay up, it's just not in him."

When we got to the fourteenth tee, Marty turned to Arnold and said, "In for a hundred?"

He laughed. "Not anymore."

"In what?" I asked.

"He wants to bet an extra hundred that I can't birdie in from here," Arnold said.

"All of them?"

"The last five."

"I take it there was a time when you made that bet."

"There was a time when I won it," he said.

As I stood on the tee with my hands in my pockets, I tried to drink in every sound, sight, and smell, so that someday I could bore my grandkids by recounting every second of the day.

Arnold birdied two of the last five and lipped out a ten-footer on eighteen that would have squared the match: He shot his age. I broke 80 and did nothing to tarnish my family name. We lost ten dollars to Jim and Marty.

As I stood on the eighteenth green shaking hands with Marty and Jim, the first thought that ran through my mind was "How could this day get any better?"

As we walked off the green, Arnold put his arm around me and said, "How 'bout coming inside and let me buy you a beer."

And so it was that I had the answer to my question.

One-Club Wonder

(or How to Save a Bundle on Caddy Fees)

N ot all world champions have major trophies on their mantels. In fact, a lot of them can walk through a thousand golf shops without being recognized. That doesn't take away from their accomplishments. The world's best dart thrower probably won't be recognized in most Irish pubs. If ESPN hadn't run out of programming, would we really know who the world's best poker player is? And perhaps more important, would we care? Some championships, even in a game like golf, are—how to put it?—more specialized than others.

One such title is the World One Club Championship. In this event, participants can pick any single club they wish as long as it conforms to USGA rules. And they have to adhere to every other rule in the book—no gimmes or generous drops. In every respect it is a championship just like any other, except that the players don't need caddies and nobody has to worry about a golf bag being plopped down in the middle of someone's backswing.

You might think the World One Club Championship is like the World of Beer Funneling Challenge, or the Pizza Palooza Championship. But some darn good players have tried their hands at winning with only one club. Scott Hoch, winner of eleven tour titles, and a guy whose brash opinions (like blasting the British Open for its slow greens and crappy weather) didn't win him a lot of friends on tour, gave the one-club thing a whirl. Bobby Clampett, a fifteen-year tour veteran who now sits in one of the CBS towers on Sunday, tried to win it, as did Jim Thorpe, the guy with sixteen wins and the dirtiest jokes on tour.

The World One Club Championship may have attracted some serious players, but when it came time to sink a must-make ten-footer with a five-iron, one player dominated the one-club format: a former N.C. State golfer who had toiled on the Australian and Asian tours before discovering his niche. His name is Thad Daber, and he is still in the *Guinness Book of World Records* as the only four-time World One Club Champion and only guy in history to shoot 68 in competition using only one golf club.

"So, what club are you playing with today?" Thad said to me after we shook hands in the parking lot of a Ben Crenshaw–designed course called Chechessee Creek.

I wasn't sure how to answer. I had never played a round with fewer than six clubs, and those were in my junior set when I was eight. It would have been easy and appropriate to say, "I don't know, you're the expert," but I figured I would get the day started right. "Well, in my experience you can get a lot of distance out of a mallet-headed putter," I said, "especially after you've missed three or four short ones."

"Six-iron," Thad said.

"Six-iron?"

"It's the shortest club you can hood down and still squeeze out a two-hundred-yard tee shot, and the longest club you can open up for a pitch."

"Six-iron it is." And we were off.

Warming up the range was pretty simple since I only had one club. Then I looked at Thad and realized how tough this was going to be. Target flags on the range were set up at 130, 155, and 190 yards, and Thad was hitting shots to every one of them. The 130-yard six-iron looked like the kind of swing you might see from a ninety-year-old man: a slow, short peck with the ball floating out like a dull pop fly. The 155-yard swing looked a lot closer to normal. He choked down on the grip and hit shots you would expect from a good player in his early forties. When it came to hitting it 190, Thad moved the ball back in his stance and hit a low hard slinger that started twenty yards right and hooked back to the target. I watched him for ten minutes, and didn't see him miss a single shot.

"I guess you have to be pretty creative, huh?" I said, wondering what I'd gotten myself into.

"In my clinics that's the one thing I tell people they can learn from this," he said. "Too many golfers have lost the art of shotmaking. Equipment's so good, you just fit the club to whatever shot you need. Playing with one club forces you to create shots, and visualize different swings."

Watching Thad left me with little optimism about my creative capacities. I could probably keep the six-iron in play from

145 to 175. But the 120 shot over a bunker was going to be a challenge.

Then I watched him hit pitches, and I realized I was really in trouble. Thad raked over a handful of balls and started taking practice swings that looked like the Nike ad with Tiger bouncing balls off a clubface. He set up so far behind the ball that he looked like he was going to step into it like a hanging curve. And the club-face was so open that all Thad could see was the shank.

Then he took a half swing, sweeping the clubhead underneath the ball and sending it spinning high in the air, a perfect flop shot. With a six-iron!

"If that's what it takes to do this, I'm in deep doodoo," I said.

"The main thing is to think about where you want to leave shots," Thad said. "Where you get killed is when you leave yourself a shot that can't be hit with a six-iron."

Watching him, I wasn't sure what that shot might be. After a dozen flop shots, he marched into the practice bunker and blasted a few over the lip onto the green. Then he said, "You should really roll a few putts before we head out."

I hung my head and slinked onto the putting green, where I spent the first ten minutes trying to figure out how to putt without whiffing or taking a divot. "Do you hit the equator of the ball with the leading edge?" I asked Thad as I hit another twelve-foot putt a total of two feet.

"I don't," he said. "But you're welcome to try that."

"Not working too well so far."

"I play the ball way back in my stance, almost behind my right foot, and then put my hands out front to de-loft the club. Then I just putt normally. You get a little jump off the clubface when you do that, but the ball rolls pretty true."

I watched him roll in two eight-footers with the same kind of stance and swing I would have used to get my ball out from under a thorn bush. But what the heck, I wasn't getting anywhere trying to top it into the hole. I moved the ball well behind my back foot and hooded the clubface down as far as I could. I took a couple of warm-up backswings, moving the club back to the ball slowly to get a feel for the stroke. Then I looked at one of the holes about fifteen feet away. The putt broke a little right to left, so I structured my stance accordingly, picked a line and speed. Then I made a stroke. And stuck the clubhead in the ground three inches behind the ball, leaving a half-moon gash in the green.

With as much cool as I could muster, I put my foot on the gaping turf wound and said, "You ready?"

"Ready when you are."

It was only after Thad turned his back and headed to the tee that I broke out the divot tool and performed emergency surgery on the putting green.

"The key to success with one club is to manipulate the tee shot so that you leave yourself a full shot into the greens," Thad said.

"Okay," I said, having no idea what he meant.

"On a three-hundred-twenty-yard par four, you want to leave yourself a full hundred-seventy to the flag so you can make your normal swing. To do that, you have to hit it one-fifty off the tee."

"What do you do when it's a four-hundred-twenty-yard hole?"

"It depends on the hole. You can't hit two six-irons that far, or at least mortals not named Tiger can't, so you have to decide how long a third shot you want and where you want to be when you hit it. If you've got a big green that's open in the front, you can hit two full shots and leave yourself a seventy- or eighty-yard chip that you can run up. If the green has a lot of bunkers, or has water in the front, you want to hit a seventy- or eighty-yard second shot so you'll have a pretty normal third shot. It's all about laying up to the distance you want for your approach."

"Thinking about your second shot before you hit your first," I said.

"It's a lost art."

It was an art I had never mastered. To prove it, on the first hole I hit a tee shot 190 yards, leaving myself the perfect distance for a full six-iron. Unfortunately, my strategy exceeded my execution, and I hit a push cut that landed in a greenside bunker.

"Tested right off the bat," Thad said.

"How do you do this again?" I asked as I climbed into the pit.

"This is where you have to be creative, and stay aware of your face angle."

"Face angle?"

"Yeah, you've got to keep the clubface open, and slice underneath it. Most people never think about their clubface, which is a real problem when you're hitting the wrong club."

"Especially if it's the only club you've got."

He shrugged and smiled. He'd seen this tried often enough to know that I had no chance.

I made what I thought was a good swing. I set up with the ball well outside my left foot and laid the clubface as open as I could.

The result was a cold shank. The ball would have run into a water hazard had it not buried under the lip of the bunker.

"I think you might want to look at some other geometric options," Thad said.

He was right. The only shot I had was to hit it away from the hole and back into the fairway, where I would at least have a chance at making double bogey.

The plan worked brilliantly until I got onto the green, where I promptly three-putted for an eight.

"Well, this is fun," I said.

"Yeah, those will kill you."

"I take it you don't make many high numbers."

"You know, in twenty years of playing with one club I've never hit a ball out of bounds, and never made more than a double bogey on any hole."

"Never?" I could barely believe what I was hearing.

"Nope."

"In how many holes?"

"Over a thousand rounds, so how many is that?"

"At least eighteen thousand," I said.

He shrugged. "That sounds about right."

"Is that in the *Guinness Book of World Records*?"

"They don't recognize that as a category."

In the sixties and seventies, when I was an enthusiastic newcomer to the game, the greatest thing you could say about a player was that he could "work" the ball, creating low, high, left, and right curving shots at will. Lanny Wadkins was a master at this; so was

Jerry Pate. The praise for shotmakers among insiders was "He can really golf his ball," which meant nothing to anyone outside the game, but everything to those inside it.

Now, it was a part of golf no one mentioned.

"We stopped thinking about working shots twenty years ago," Thad said. "Metal woods and hard golf balls killed it. Working the ball requires spin. In today's game you want to do whatever you can not to spin it."

"It doesn't take long for you to forget that you're playing with one club, because you're so focused on the shot you've got to hit next," I said, which seemed crazy. If I hadn't been playing with one club I wouldn't have needed to manufacture shots. Because I was limited to a single weapon, I had to think two and three shots ahead and plan what I needed to do to get it close. This was what golf was like before engineers and computer technicians sucked the soul out of shotmaking.

Thad was nodding before I finished my thought. "That's another thing I tell the students at my clinics. Nobody expects you to play competitively with one club. But everybody should play one round every couple of months this way. It changes your perspective: improves how you think your way around the course."

"Is six-iron the club of choice for everybody?" I asked.

"No, it takes practice to see what club best suits your game. I think Jim Thorpe played the championship with a seven-iron, but he hits it so hard he could hood it down and get a lot of distance. Some guys go with five-iron, although I think you have a hard time hitting short shots with something that straight-faced."

"How long did it take you to settle on six-iron?"

"I made that decision pretty quick," he said. "I've never been a bomber, which was one of the reasons I never went very far as a tour player. Then the first time I tried to hit a soft pitch with a five-iron I realized I needed something a little shorter and more lofted."

"So, you picked up the six-iron and hit flop shots right away."

"That one takes some time, but it gets lots of applause when I hit it in front of a crowd."

By the seventh hole I had figured out the laying-up-to-your-number thing, but it didn't matter because I was three- and four-putting every green. I think the mortal wound I inflicted on the practice putting green had scared me out of digging chunks in Crenshaw's crowned masterpieces. As I stood over ten-footers my trusty six-iron started looking more and more like a plowshare.

"Who would have thought putting would be the hardest part of this?"

"Anybody who's tried it," Thad said. "The beauty of playing with one club is that you can pretty much throw conventional technique out the window, even in putting."

"Especially in putting," I said.

"But it takes your focus away from the swing or the stroke. It makes you concentrate on doing whatever it takes to get the ball in the hole. Unless they've changed the rules since I last checked, that is the objective."

He was right: There is no place on the scorecard for commentary: just little boxes for numbers. On the final hole, I shut the face of my six-iron and hooked a tee shot one pace north of 200 yards. Then I hit a six-iron onto the front apron of the green. I chipped with a six-iron to within three feet, and didn't come close to hitting the hole with my putt for par.

"Oh!" Thad said as I tapped in. "I was really hoping you'd make that."

"Why?" I said. "What in my performance today would lead you to believe that I would?"

"Nothing really," he said. "But I wanted you to make it so you could say you broke ninety."

My jaw dropped. "You mean I shot ninety?"

"Afraid so." Then he opened his arms like a game show host selling the consolation prize. "But wasn't it fun?"

I had to concede that point. Score aside, playing with one club was one of the most enjoyable rounds of golf I'd had in a while.

"Most fun you can have playing like an eighteen handicapper," I said.

"Keep playing, you'll get better."

"Thad, you don't need to worry about me," I said. "I'll always keep playing. But as far as I'm concerned, your world records are safe."

THIRTEEN

Shooting 80 with Mr. 59

(or Don't Worry, Only Three People Have Done It
in Thirty Years)

It's not often that winning the Danny Thomas Memphis Classic makes you more famous than winning the PGA Championship. But then it's not every day you become the first man to shoot 59 on the PGA Tour. Such was the case for Allen Lee "Al" Geiberger, who not only won a major championship in 1966, but also racked up ten other tour titles including the Tournament of Champions and the Players Championship, as well as ten wins on the Champions Tour. Al also played on two Ryder Cup teams, amassing a 5-1-3 record, but all those victories pale in comparison to the one round in the sweltering delta that forever defined Al's career.

Al Geiberger is golf's equivalent of Roger Bannister, a noted neurologist who did breakthrough work in the field of autonomic failures; served as the first chairman on the English Sports Council; and was the first person in sports to institute testing for anabolic steroids, work that earned him a knighthood in 1975. Unfortunately, nobody remembers any of that. For the rest of history Sir Roger Bannister will be known as the first runner to break the four-minute mile. Likewise, Al Geiberger will, for as long as people play golf, be known as "Mr. 59," the first man to break 60 in a sanctioned event.

Al was sixty-nine years old and staring headlong at the thirtieth anniversary of his historic round when I got an invitation to play with him in Palm Desert, California. The invite came from a guy named Ted Lennon, the developer of Stone Eagle, another expensive golf enclave in the arid Coachella Valley, a rocky strip of hostile earth that even the Indians wouldn't settle. Stone Eagle sits on a boulder-strewn hillside that was once a training ground for Patton's Third Army before Ole Blood and Guts plowed through North Africa.

Ted had hired Al as goodwill golf ambassador for the club. I was among a group of freeloading golf writers lured to the desert to see the place under the guise of playing with Mr. 59.

My pal and fellow golf freak Larry Olmsted, whom I hadn't seen since the debacle at Doonbeg, was part of the junket, along with a couple of writers from *Golfweek,* and the guy who heads up the course rating panel for *Golf Magazine.* Larry had just returned from a wine and golf tour of Portugal, and was heading straight from Palm Springs to Honolulu, where he planned to run a marathon on Maui and play half a dozen courses as part of a lifestyle feature for *US Airways* magazine.

"You're my idol," I said to Larry.

"My wife doesn't share your admiration."

As our driver delivered us into the parking lot at Stone Eagle, I looked at the rock-strewn hillsides and verbalized the question that was on everyone's mind. "Not to be obtuse, but where's the golf course?"

"You can't see it from here," the driver said.

"You can't see the golf course from the clubhouse?"

"The course is pretty isolated."

Even though the surrounding hills looked like a great spot for Clint Eastwood to be ambushed by the Apaches, I figured the golf course was close and in a serene setting. Even when I saw that the golf carts had custom suspensions and high-clearance all-terrain tires, I didn't panic. Sometimes rough was rough. A little off-roading never hurt anybody.

It wasn't until we struck out for the grill room that my pucker reflex kicked into high gear. Hairpin turns in a top-heavy golf cart aren't much fun under normal circumstances. When we rounded the last curve before reaching the restaurant, I stared over the corner of the cart path into a canyon, and my mind flashed back to that movie scene where Butch and Sundance jumped off a Bolivian cliff.

"The view's spectacular, isn't it?"

My chauffeur, John Fitzpatrick, was the marketing director, and as such, he was obliged to point out every vista on the property by waving his arm like Monty Hall pointing to door number three. If I'd known him longer than five minutes I would have screamed, "Two hands, John! Ten and two! Safety first!" Instead, I gave a quick "Uh-huh," and grabbed the oh-shit handle on the roof of the cart.

Once we stopped and my legs quit shaking I was able to focus on something other than the cart path. That's when I realized John was right: The golf course stretching out in front of us looked like a bomber squadron had dropped a zillion rolls of green carpet into the canyon.

"It's something, isn't it?" That question came from behind me, a voice I didn't recognize. When I turned, I saw Al Geiberger staring at the scene behind me.

"I never get tired of looking at it," Al said. "At different times of day the sun hits the mountains just right. You can't believe how beautiful it is."

"Al should know," John Fitzpatrick said. "He's out here almost every day."

"Not quite, but I can't get enough of it."

The sales pitch continued through lunch where the menu included a peanut butter and jelly sandwich called the "Mr. 59," which Al claimed was the best in the valley. "Nobody appreciates a good peanut butter and jelly sandwich anymore," he said. "Once you have this one, you'll never be able to make one again." We all passed, but he earned an A for effort. It wasn't until we got onto the golf course that I realized the pitch for the PBJ was just Al's way of clearing his throat. Throughout the day he sold us on the shot values of the golf course, the beauty of the real estate, the character of the owners, the views, the shadows, the food; he even tried to convince us that you could walk Stone Eagle, which was technically true in the sense that you could hike the Andes if you set your mind to it.

"You'll find the landing areas are very generous," Al said. "But you have to be in the right spot on the greens. Like on the first hole here, you can't hit it at the flag. You've got to be right of the hole, or the ball will roll all the way off the green."

And so it went for the entire round. "This is a great little par three," he said as we climbed to the third tee, a trek that winded me, but that Al seemed to hop up without any problem. "Your eye tells you to hit it right at the hole, but everything slopes right. You want to be left of the hole."

He proceeded to hit a solid seven-iron ten feet from the flag.

"Just like that, huh," I said.

"You can go a little farther left than that."

"I was kidding, Al."

"Take your time. Hit a good one."

Five holes into the round and between sales pitches, Al pointed a finger at me and said, "You know I've been trying to think of who you remind me of, and it just came to me. You look like an old pro named Mark Pfeil. You even swing like him."

"Oh, wow," I said. "I know Mark Lyle."

"No, not Mark Lyle: Mark Pfeil, a Southern California guy who tried to play the tour for a while. He didn't make it, but he still plays well around here."

"He couldn't make it, huh?"

"He bounced back and forth for a while, never really made it on tour."

"Swing like him, do I?"

"It's uncanny. I wish I had some photos."

"I'll take your word for it."

It wasn't until the sixth hole that the subject of the 59 came up. Al and I both made birdie on the short par four. He patted me on the back and said, "Don't ever give up, because you never know what's coming next. When I shot fifty-nine, I started the day seven shots back of a guy named Tom Storey from Las Vegas. He shot sixty-five in the first round. We were out at the same time on Friday, and I think he shot seventy. He played pretty good again. He got in and I was three shots ahead of him."

I saw this as the perfect opening, so I said, "Al, are you surprised that after thirty years only three people have matched your fifty-nine and nobody's broken it?"

Chip Beck shot 59 in 1991 during the Las Vegas Invitational at Sunrise Golf Club, and David Duval did it in the 1999 Bob Hope Classic at PGA West. On the LPGA side Annika Sorenstam shot 59 at Moon Valley Country Club in Phoenix in 2001 to set the women's mark, but according to those who know, Al's 59 on a soggy 7,249-yard course in Memphis in the era of wooden clubs and rubber golf balls was the most impressive.

"I guess I'm a little surprised," he said. "Every time somebody gets close, my phone starts ringing. I'll talk for a while, and then whoever's up there will make a couple of pars or a bogey and the story's over."

"I figured it would be like the four-minute mile," I said. "I thought once you broke the psychological barrier, a lot of people would shoot in the fifties."

He smiled and shook his head. "I'm always asked, 'Why hasn't anyone broken it, yet? Why can't anybody shoot fifty-eight?' I don't really know, but I heard Jim Colbert say that it's a long way from sixty to fifty-nine, and an even longer trip from fifty-nine to fifty-eight. That's as good an answer as any."

Larry jumped in, saying, "I'm betting you've got one of the longest unbroken streaks in the *Guinness Book of World Records*."

"I haven't checked, but you're probably right."

"I have," Larry said.

I stepped away from my shot and said, "Larry, you read the *Guinness Book of World Records*?"

"I check to make sure I'm still in it."

"You have a world record?"

He nodded and said, "I played poker for seventy-two straight hours. The record's still standing."

Wind whistled across the boulders as I pondered what to say next, but Al beat me to it. "Why would you do such a thing?" he said.

"Hey, you're 'Mr. 59.' I wanted to be 'Mr. Poker.'"

We were quiet for a second. Then Al said, "This is a good par three. I'm hitting four-iron, if that helps."

Al's knees keep him off the Champions Tour these days. As long as the old guys were using carts he was winning. When the commissioner decided that seniors should walk the courses like everyone else, Al was forced into retirement. By the time tour rule-makers realized that walking wasn't so necessary for guys with arthritis and heart conditions, Al had been out of competition so long he simply didn't go back. "I didn't want to embarrass myself," he said.

Still, he was a long way from embarrassment. He was even par on a very difficult golf course, and hitting it past two guys who were younger than his eldest son.

"Who knows, Al, you might have another fifty-nine in you," I said.

"You know, after that round my caddy, who was a crusty old guy named Len Lynch, said, 'If he'd listened to me, we'd have shot fifty-seven.' He was a beauty, one of those surly career caddies who stayed out there forever. Nobody could keep him for more than a couple of years, because he drove you nuts. He didn't have any teeth: mumbled all the time. Plus, he made up words. Pensacola, Florida, was Pepsi-Cola, Florida; Gibby Gilbert was Gilby. The best one, though, was when we played this one hole where the landscape ran one way, but the green sloped the other. Len pulled me aside and said, 'This looks like it goes right, but the grass goes underneath like; it's one of them optional illusions.' I've used that one a lot since then."

By then we were on the eighteenth hole, and Mr. 59 was one-under-par. A birdie and he would shoot his age.

"This is a tough tee shot," he said. "The hole's long, and you have to hit it down there where you have a level lie. I try to put a little extra into this one and sling it off the hillside."

The swing Larry and I saw that day hadn't changed in thirty years, and Al still has a little extra when he needs it. His tee shot on eighteen started out to the right and drew back, hitting a slope and bounding forward. When it came to a stop the sixty-nine-year-old had hit a 315-yard drive.

"You killed it, Al," I said.

He smiled, and said, "I can still move it when I need it."

He made bogey on the last hole to shoot even par, a number that would still earn a decent check on the Champions Tour. But Al said he was content to watch his kids and grandkids; his fifteen-year-old daughter, Kathleen, was a star volleyball player, and Al was going straight from the course to watch her practice. He also seemed content playing golf with prospective members at Stone Eagle.

"It's a beautiful golf course, isn't it?" he said as we finished.

"Great, Al," I said, speaking more of the company than the setting. "It was great."

"Mark Pfeil," he said, pointing his finger at me again.

"The guy that couldn't quite make it."

"I'm going to check the house and see if I have any pictures of him. You'll be surprised."

"No more so than I have been already," I said.

FOURTEEN

Eye to Eye with the Golf Freek

(or Where Did That One Go?)

I can hit a golf ball pretty well standing on my knees. It took some practice, and way too much spare time, but there's no better way to win a bet than hitting a 200-yard tee shot from a communion kneel. I've also hit plenty of balls one-handed. I will still hit a dozen or so practice shots with only my left hand, just to make sure I feel my left side leading the swing. I also hit wedge shots with just my right hand when working on high pitches. On the golf course, I've hit enough left-handed shots to feel confident flipping a seven-iron upside down and swinging from the wrong side of the ball, especially after my errant drives wind up in funky places. I've played when it was so cold I couldn't feel my hands and feet. And I've practiced while wearing earplugs and noise-canceling headphones to drown out the chatter of my fellow range rats.

But nothing I have ever done in golf could prepare me for my round in Nashville. I was headed to Spring House Golf Club, the course associated with Opryland. Nothing special about the place, unless you count the fact that it once hosted the Nashville Senior Tour event, but my playing partner for the day, the guy I had made the trip to meet, was the sort of champion who gave me the jitters even before I met him, not because of his fame—like most people, I'd never heard of the guy before doing a little research— but because of how he played.

I knew he would be easy to spot, so I hung out in the golf shop, waggling clubs until I saw him walk through the front door. There were two men, as I knew there would be, one leading the other through the clubhouse foyer and into the golf shop where I waited with a knot in my stomach.

"David," I said as they got closer.

The smaller of the two men gave me a huge smile. "I recognize that voice," he said. "You must be Steve."

I shook his outstretched hand. The smaller man, David Meador, introduced me to the other guy, Everett Davis, his coach, as David called him. Everett unclasped his hand from David's in order to shake mine. All the while, David faced the grill room, his eyes drawn to the sounds of chattering golfers having breakfast before their rounds.

But his eyes were unseeing. David Meador is blind. He is also a champion golfer, winning the United States Blind Golf Association Championship at famed Firestone Country Club in Akron, Ohio, the site of the World Golf Championships Bridgestone Invitational, as well as the 1960, 1966, and 1975 PGA Championships.

In other words, it's a big honkin' test of golf for someone playing with all their senses. David Meador won his championship at Firestone without seeing a shot.

"Have you ever played with a blind golfer?" David asked as the staff loaded us onto the carts.

"Never had the privilege," I said. "But I'm looking forward to it, and to maybe giving it a try."

David smiled again. "Good luck with that," he said.

On the first tee, Everett, who turned out to be far more than what you would normally lump into the broad definition of a "coach," escorted David to the tee, put the ball on the peg for him, and lined him up by pointing the shaft of the club down the target line. David reached out and felt the club. Then he positioned his chest against it so that his shoulders and feet were aligned.

"Good," Everett said as he handed David the club. David gripped it as any golfer would, but Everett held on to the clubhead until David gave him the go-ahead nod, the same sort of subtle signal I'd seen rodeo cowboys give the guys manning bull-riding chutes. Everett placed the clubhead directly behind the ball, and said "Okay, David."

As Everett cleared the tee, David made a smooth, technically proficient swing that sent his opening tee shot straight down the fairway. It wasn't long, maybe 230 yards, but he hit it better than 85 percent of the guys with perfect eyesight waiting to tee off behind us.

Then the fun started. I reached into my golf bag and pulled out a sleeping mask. "I'm going to give this a whirl," I said.

Everett laughed out loud. "Okay," he said. "We'll see."

I put the mask on while I was still standing by the golf cart, which meant I needed help getting up the hill to the first tee. But having never been blind, I didn't realize how much help I needed. I grabbed my driver (the longest club in my bag and an easy find with or without vision) and marched up the hill on my own.

"You're going the wrong way," Everett said.

I turned and headed in the other direction.

"No, you need to stop," Everett said. "Remember, you're on a golf course. You never know when you might be walking into a hazard and about to trip on something. Just wait and I'll help you."

"As a past champion I serve on the competitions committee for the U.S. Blind Golf Association," David said. "We had an issue not long ago where some people charged one woman of being sighted. So, we debated what to do about it, and finally I said, 'The next event's in Florida. Why don't we have a coach walk her a few feet from an alligator and see how she responds?' Blind humor."

Just then I felt a hand on my arm. "Here, grab this club." Everett led my hand to the grip end of my driver. Standing there in total darkness I didn't have any choice but to do as he said, so I held the club. Then he said, "I'm going to lead you now," which he did. When the club stopped, I assumed we were somewhere near the tee markers.

I felt hands grab my shoulders and turn me in the right direction. "Just relax while I line you up," Everett said as he manipulated my shoulders and hips. "Okay, now I'm going to hold a club in front of you, just like I did for David, and I want you to reach out and touch it with both hands."

Again I did as I was told, extending my arms until I felt the club. By this time claustrophobia had set in. Not only was I out of sorts being blind, I was getting dizzy from all this walking around in the dark.

"Now slowly step forward until you're lined up with the club," Everett said.

I slid my feet forward a half step, and did my best to set up in something resembling my normal stance.

"Good," Everett said. "Now grip the club." He put the grip of the driver in my left hand, and I found my normal grip. "And I'm going to put the club behind the ball for you." I felt the clubhead move down to the ground. "Okay, I'm going to step away now. You can swing when you're ready."

I went through my normal pre-shot routine which included waggling the club back and forth behind the ball a couple of times.

"Oops."

"What?" I said.

"You just knocked the ball off the tee."

"Oh."

"It's best if you don't move the club after I put it down behind the ball. Without a visual reference, it's hard to get it back."

"Got it. Sorry."

"No problem," Everett said as he grabbed the clubhead and slowly set it behind the ball again. "Okay, whenever you're ready."

I started the pre-shot routine again, only this time without the clubhead waggle. I still moved my feet and head a little, which prompted Everett to chuckle.

"What?" I said, sensing that I might have a kick-me sign on my shirt or something.

"Nothing," he said, still trying to suppress a snicker. "You just looked down the target line. I was going to remind you that you can't see."

"Thanks, Everett."

"Whenever you're ready."

I set up without any more waggling gyrations and started my swing. Within the first nanosecond all the assumptions I had developed about my own game scurried away. Throughout my life I had always considered myself to be someone who sensed his own golf swing not through technical analysis, but through an elevated sense of feel, the delicate hands of a surgeon, that sort of thing. I had also said "I could hit that shot in my sleep," more times than I could count. Well, unless I was sleeping with my eyes open, I realized that all the things I thought I knew about myself were wrong.

At the top of the backswing, a position I had been in more than a million times in my life, I was sure I would fall down. I had no balance and my head was spinning like New Year's morning. Once I started the downswing, instinct kicked in and I finished . . . and heard the sickening *whish* of club passing over ball: a complete whiff.

This was followed by the awkward silence.

"You can laugh, guys. It's okay."

"I would, but I didn't see it," David said.

I laughed at that one, and Everett blew air over his lips like a motorboat, releasing the pent-up guffaw he'd been holding since my whiff.

"Let's give it another try," Everett said. He reset me to the target line and went through the same routine, setting the club behind the ball and telling me to fire when ready.

This time I focused on staying down and through the shot. The result was the club hitting the ground a foot behind the ball. Had it not been a driver, I would have whiffed again. Thankfully, the sole plate of a 460cc titanium Cobra is so big that it bounces like a 747 without wheels. The clubface ricocheted into the ball, sending it and several clumps of dirt somewhere off the front of the tee.

"Umm," Everett said.

I could stand it no longer. I ripped the blindfold off and said, "Where'd it go?"

"Left," Everett said. "Over the mound. We might find it."

"Sorry, I won't be much help," David said.

"You know, David, I didn't expect you'd be quite this funny."

"I lost my eyesight, not my sense of humor."

David wasn't born blind. As he explained to me, not only was he a kid with great eyesight, he had been a ball-hawking caddy when he was young. His first experience in golf had been when he was ten years old. A swaggering gambler named Floyd Fox showed up for his regular game and David, who was sitting outside the clubhouse hoping to pick up some spending money, said, "Hey, Floyd, you want a caddy?" The precociousness caught Floyd off guard, and he hired David.

"We got along fine until he got three down," David said.

"Then he handed me three balls and said, 'Go wash these.' I ran off to the ball washer and stuffed the balls inside. Then I realized there was a wooden paddle with holes in it where the balls were supposed to fit. I spent the next five minutes with my little arm down inside the ball washer fishing out Floyd's balls."

That wasn't his only gaffe on the bag. Once he became a seasoned eleven-year-old caddy, he carried for his dad, who was a mid-range player at their Southern Illinois club. During one of his first rounds as his father's looper, David stepped back to help line up a putt and fell backwards into a sand trap, landing on his rump in a pile of white powder. When he crawled out, his dad and the two men in his group were doubled over in laughter.

"I just wish I'd been quick enough to say, 'It breaks six inches to the left,'" he said.

David graduated to playing with his father as a teenager, and became good enough that he had a couple of holes-in-one. His father nicknamed him "Ace."

"So, how'd you lose your eyesight?" I asked.

"Car crash. Head hit the dash."

He expanded on that story later in the day. David had just graduated from high school in 1966 and was working as a dispatcher for his local police department. After finishing his 4:00 P.M.–to–midnight shift, he had gone out on the "alley patrol" with the third-shift patrolman. A few minutes after one in the morning, a '62 Impala sped through a traffic light and the patrolman hit the lights. When the car sped up and tried to outrun them, David and the patrolman went in hot pursuit. The result was a crashed patrol car and a blind teenager.

"Golf didn't come up again for a while," he said.

When it did, David played with some buddies from work with the assistance of a teenaged "coach." His game consisted of hitting a few practice balls in a nearby park two or three times a week, and playing early on Saturday mornings. "After a while I got pretty good," he said.

I was still having trouble grasping just how big a role visual acuity played in balance, timing, walking, and even standing. I hadn't whiffed a tee shot in forty years, and I was only forty-four years old!

"I can't believe how hard this is," I said to Everett as I put the mask back on and shuffled through the rough to my ball.

"It makes you appreciate what guys like David are able to do."

"And what you do," I said. "You've got more patience than I knew existed in one person."

He grabbed my shoulders again and said, "Okay, here's the club. Go ahead and set up."

My blind-golfer game could not have gotten much worse. I shanked the first iron shot I hit. Then I whiffed another one. The first shot to connect with the clubface using something other than a driver was a cold top that rolled about twenty yards down the fairway. Then I got on the green, and the fun really started.

"Okay, hold my elbow, and we'll step off the distance of the putt," Everett said.

Again, I did as I was told, holding his arm as we paced off the putt. It was five paces, a fifteen-footer, give or take a few inches.

"Feel good about the distance?" he asked.

"Got it."

"Okay, I'm going to line you up again, just like before." We went through the same routine with the club. But I felt pretty good about this. I had always been a good putter (except the day I putted with a six-iron) and I knew I could stroke a fifteen-footer with my eyes closed. I'd hit practice putts with my eyes shut before, and I'd putted while looking at the hole instead of the ball to help my feel. This was going to be a piece of cake.

"Ready when you are," Everett said when he had my putter on the ground behind the ball.

I relaxed my grip pressure, forward-pressed my hands, which was my normal trigger to begin the stroke, and hit what I thought was a great putt.

"Whoa," Everett said. "You're twenty feet past the hole."

"What?"

"Take my arm, and I'll show you." So we walked the five paces to the hole, and another seven to where my ball had come to rest.

"Not quite so hard this time," he said.

After we went through the setup routine, I hit a much softer putt, or so I thought. I was shocked when David said, "Oh, no, that's way too hard."

"Dude, you're blind."

"Yeah, but I'm not deaf."

"Where's that one, Everett?"

"Ten feet by."

David chuckled. "Told you."

I played three holes with the stupid mask on my face. It took an hour and a half, and I lost nine golf balls. When I finally cried uncle, I watched David play the rest of the round with more awe and appreciation than I'd had for any golfer I'd ever seen. Sure, Tiger did amazing things: things that I had never seen anyone else do with a golf ball. But he had all his senses. Put him in a blindfold, and my guess is Tiger would look as lost and helpless as the rest of us. When I saw David hit a perfect 150-yard six-iron pin high, fifteen feet left of the hole on eighteen, I thought it was the greatest shot I'd ever seen in golf.

"What do you normally shoot, David?" I said.

"Well, if you break a hundred in blind golf, you're really doing something."

"If you break a hundred in regular golf you're better than two thirds of the people who play."

"True."

"So, I take it you break a hundred quite a bit."

"More than most," he said with a grin.

He two-putted the final green for a bogey in one of the most impressive and humbling games I'd ever had the pleasure of playing.

A few minutes later the waitress brought us lunch and told David where his utensils and drink were. "David," I said, "the biggest thing for me was the blackness. The absence of seeing anything was disorienting. Do you see anything?"

"Oh sure," he said. "If you've ever looked through a kaleidoscope, that's what I see, swirling colors that pop out all the time. Some days there are more colors and more movement than others, but I always see something. It's quite beautiful, really."

Then he said, "You know, I won the U.S. Blind Golf Championship in a playoff. I shot forty-five on the back nine at Firestone, and actually parred the par-five sixteenth, the hole they call 'The Monster,' and the eighteenth. That got me into a playoff with Pat Browne of New Orleans, who is an incredible player. In the playoff on the first hole, I hit my second shot in a greenside bunker. I didn't know it at the time, but the lip of that bunker was over six feet high. Even if I'd been sighted, I wouldn't have been able to see the flag. My coach didn't tell me what kind of shot I had. He just said, 'Dave, you need to hit it a little harder than normal.'

"I did, and hit it eight feet past the hole. It was only then that my coach handed me the grip end of the sand wedge and walked me to the front of the bunker. The lip was well over my head. So, we climbed out and two-putted for bogey to win the championship."

"Did you say anything to your coach about not telling you what kind of bunker shot you had?" I asked.

David shook his head. "He told me everything I needed to know." Then he tapped his finger on the table and paused, obviously reliving a fond memory.

"You know," he said. "If you can't see the trouble that's in front of you, you can't be intimidated by it."

"I hope you don't mind if I use that line."

"Not as long as you tell everybody where you heard it."

FIFTEEN

Age and Talent vs. Long-Haired Youth and Freeloading

(or If You Can't Shoot Your Age, What Are You Doing Out Here?)

It had been a long time since I'd been called a "young man," especially on the golf course, where my long gray locks glistened like Christmas tree tinsel. I'm closer to my father's age than my children's, a fact crystallized by the teenagers at my home club who insist on calling me "sir" and "mister." That was why it caught me off guard when the final champion on my world champion tour said, "How are you today, young fellow?"

"Thank you, Leo," I said to Leo Luken, the tall old man with a strong handshake and clear voice whom I met outside the golf shop at Palmetto Dunes Resort on Hilton Head. "If youth is a state of mind, I'm a whippersnapper, but I'm not sure anybody else lumps me in the 'young man' category."

"When you get to my age, you're pretty safe calling everybody young," Leo said. At eighty-eight, Leo had outlived all his elders and most of his peers. He could call me whatever he wanted; I was young enough to be his grandson.

"I'm happy you were able to come down," he said. "We're going to have a good time."

I felt fortunate to be playing with Leo, not because of his advanced age—he had the kind of spring in his step that said "I'm not going anywhere for a while"—but because the round with him was not why I had gone to Hilton Head in the first place. In fact, before heading down to coastal South Carolina, I didn't know who Leo Luken was.

My original plan had been to write about the excesses of golf development in the coastal South. Myrtle Beach alone offered a thousand holes of cheap golf, a big-ass water park, the former home base of Hooters Air—wings, beer, and tight T-shirts at 40,000 feet—that would have made a great fictional setting for a Coen brothers film (except that it was real) and the you've-gotta-be-kidding-me truck stop, "South of the Border," a Tijuana-themed gas-and-go with a giant statue of its mascot "Pedro," marking the exit off I-95.

Farther south, Hilton Head was a twelve-by-three-mile island, and, prior to 1958, an age when "low country" carried social as well as geographic connotations, only accessible by boat. Back then, water oaks stretched upward and outward like fat men yawning on their porch swings while pelicans and gulls swooped and swirled over marshy wetland fields. The smell of shrimp and clams wafted through the salt-filled air, and the communal sounds of low country boils where steel kettles stewed shellfish, corn, okra, and potatoes, drifted out with the tide. What few roads existed were made of sand and shale.

Ninety percent of the residents were black, descendants of slaves who had retained the social and cultural traits of their ancestors, even to the point of speaking a mixture of African languages and Elizabethan English known as Gullah. Most fished or shrimped for a living, while others lived off the land, hunting and growing whatever they needed. It was a world that most had never seen until 1986, when it was boxed up tight and wrapped with a bow in *The Prince of Tides,* the wildly popular Pat Conroy novel.

Today, Hilton Head has twenty-six golf courses, 360 restaurants, twenty-nine hotels, five marinas, and 40,000 residents (mostly white) living in gated communities islanders call—honest to god, I'm not making this up—"Plantations." If that weren't in-your-face enough, each plantation on Hilton Head is managed by a "regime." And, yes, they wear seersucker. There is also a Wal-Mart at "mid-island" fronted by a Cracker Barrel, and an outlet mall greeting visitors as they cross the crowded bridge connecting Hilton Head with a booming mainland. There are ninety real estate offices, nineteen time-share developers, and one alarmingly ugly four-lane expressway called the "cross-island connector" that juts out into the salt water. Harbour Towne, the most famous area on the island because of an annual PGA Tour stop, is a faux village with a fake lighthouse and Ye Olde English spelling on shops, streets, and condos that are neither old nor English. Every year 1.4 million rounds of golf are played on Hilton Head.

With an infrastructure bursting at the seams, golf development has spewed over into the outer reaches of Beaufort County. Today, the hole-in-the-wall communities of Bluffton, Spring Island, and Daufuskie (an island accessible only by water taxi that now has five golf courses on three plantations) are in a race to see who can rape the landscape fastest. Daufuskie, the remote island depicted in one of Conroy's earlier novels, *The Water Is Wide,* gets its name phonetically by being the first key island in the South Carolina chain. If you can imagine one of the old black Gullah-speaking residents telling a khaki-clad white newcomer in boat shoes that he is standing on "the first key," you see how Daufuskie got its name.

The perfect encapsulation of the state of things on Hilton Head, and Southern Coastal America in general, was a conversation I had with Harold, the former owner of Harold's Restaurant, a small brick building behind a Shell gas station in the middle of the island. Hamburgers at Harold's are thick, greasy, and served with fried eggs, fatback pork, and hot sauce. And when Harold spoke, you could not distinguish between the words "golf course," and "Gulf Coast." Both come out as "guffcoas." After chatting with him for a few minutes, I realized that the "guffcoas" (golf course) had led Harold to decide to uproot his family and move to the "guffcoas" (Gulf Coast). He'd seen enough. A hundred years of history be damned; Harold was not staying any longer.

But as ripe as Hilton Head seemed for a good reaming, I discovered an even better story when a friend of mine who lived on the island said, "Why don't you play a round of golf with Leo Luken?"

My response was, "Who is Leo Luken?"

"He's the World 'Shoot Your Age' Champion," Brad said. "The guy has shot his age more than five hundred times. They held a championship down in Florida and he won the thing by shooting six shots under his age. He beat Arnold Palmer, Gary Player, everybody."

And so it was that I found myself on the first tee of the Robert Trent Jones Course at Palmetto Dunes with a gray-haired great-grandfather who was working the hustle before I put a peg in the ground.

"Give me fourteen shots, and I'll play you for five bucks three ways," Leo said.

"Fourteen shots! Leo, I don't even know you."

"I'm eighty-eight years old. What's to know? I've got to break ninety and live till the end of the round to have a shot."

"Good point. Okay, a five-dollar Nassau."

"Press is optional if you're two down."

"Why do I get the feeling I'm being snookered?"

"Just play well. We're going have a great time."

I knew I was in trouble on the first tee when Leo stripped a drive down the middle, hit a short iron to the front of the green, and casually two-putted for a par (net birdie) to go one up.

"How many times have you shot your age?" I asked as he headed to two.

"Five hundred sixty-eight as of this morning."

"That's unbelievable," I said, shaking my head.

There are a couple of gold standards in golf. One is shooting a 59, something that's only happened three times in the sixty-year history of the PGA Tour and only once on the LGPA. The other is shooting your age, a feat that anybody can accomplish as long as you retain your ability to shoot under par (assuming you ever had it in the first place) after you go on Social Security. Shooting your age one time in your life is an accomplishment worthy of a free dinner and a framed scorecard. Doing it twice puts you in elite company. Shoot your age a dozen times, and you qualify as an athletic marvel, like the eighty-year-old Iron Man triathlete or that guy who climbed Everest with no legs. Leo had shot his age more times than Mickey Mantle hit home runs.

"Yeah, Gary Player thought I was lying," Leo said. "Before we teed off the first day down at the championship, he was walking around introducing himself and asking guys how many times they'd shot their age. One guy said twelve, and another said thirty. When he got to me I said five hundred twenty-nine, which was the number at that time. Player threw up his arms and said, 'Get outta here.'" Then with a grin, Leo said, "The next day I made it five-thirty and won the tournament."

The inaugural Shoot Your Age Championship, put on by The Villages, a Lake County, Florida, retirement community, was held in May 2006. CBS aired it, and Arnie, who broke his age by three shots, finished second, three shots behind Leo.

"It was a thrill," Leo said. "Arnie was one of the first people out on the last green to congratulate me, which was wonderful, because many years before, when Arnie was just a kid, I took a golf lesson from his dad, Deacon. I got to tell him about it, and he spent the rest of the evening saying, 'You know, Leo took lessons from my father.' Well, it wasn't really lessons, but I let it go. Arnie was almost as proud of me winning the thing after I told him about his dad as he would have been if he'd won it himself."

Leo went two up with another net birdie on the third. He wasn't wasting much time bearing out my theory about being hustled.

"So, I guess that's one of the biggest thrills of your life," I said, attempting to move the conversation forward and get Leo's mind off schooling me like a hapless rookie.

"Oh, no," he said. "I'm a member of the National Softball Hall of Fame."

Before I could ask, he reached into a pouch and produced a ring the size of my cell phone. Sure enough, it was from the ASA National Softball Hall of Fame. Leo was inducted in 1993.

"What position did you play?"

"I was a pitcher in a fast-pitch league. Played for twenty-two years in Kentucky and Indiana."

"Did you win three hundred games?"

"Oh no, I won five hundred eleven."

"Five hundred eleven games!"

"Yeah, of course that was over twenty-two years. I was working for fourteen dollars a week as a kid, and realized that I could pick up some extra money if I played for one of the industrial teams."

"Five hundred eleven games."

"Uh-huh. From 1944 till July of 1946 I won fifty-three in a row. I finally lost one in July of '46, and then won a dozen more."

"How fast could you hurl it?"

"I was getting clocked at over a hundred miles an hour. My fastest I think was one-oh-four."

"With a softball?"

He looked at me like I was dense. "That's right," he said slowly.

Through the next six holes, as Leo won the front nine two up, I learned that the man known in softball circles as "Leo the Lion Hearted" started his career by racking up a 42-6 record for the Nick Carr Boosters of Covington, Kentucky. He was the team leader when they won the 1939 ASA national title. The team they beat that year (and the one Leo beat seven times) was the Zollner Pistons of Fort Wayne, Indiana. The next year, Fred Zollner hired Leo for the piston plant and put him on the mound for his softball team, where Leo went 12-0 in national championship play, throwing a no-hitter in the deciding game of the championship series in 1942. And in 1949, he had 151 strikeouts in 145 innings.

"I'm also in the Kentucky and Indiana sports halls of fame," he said.

"Leo, you could be the only guy in history who's a world champion in one sport and in the Hall of Fame in another," I said.

"I also taught ballroom dancing for twenty years," he said. "My wife and I danced for three hours a night, six nights a week for twenty years to make extra money for the kids."

"How many kids?"

"Six. I'm a lot prouder of them than I am of this shoot-your-age title or being in these halls of fame. My daughter Lisa was named Student Athlete of the Decade at Purdue for the eighties. That means a lot more to me than anything I've done."

"Is your wife still alive?"

He got a faraway look, and his face tightened as he stared at an egret wading through one of the lagoons. "Yeah, but she's having a hard time. We've been married sixty-four years. That's another thing: I'd give back this ring and all those titles if you could promise me we'd make it to sixty-five."

We played the next two holes in total silence except for an occasional "good shot" or "nice putt," which I seemed to be saying a lot.

Finally, after he got me one down on the back, I asked him, "So, Leo, what's the secret to shooting your age?"

"Well, the first trick is to live long enough to have a chance to do it. Until you get to sixty-five, you're going to struggle."

"When did you do it for the first time?"

"I shot seventy-one in a Tennessee amateur event when I was seventy-one years old. I guess that was seventeen years ago now. Time flies when you're having fun."

"So did the floodgates open after that?"

"No, doing it the first hundred times was pretty tough. After that it got easier."

"Okay, other than having enough birthdays and staying upright, what else do you have to do?"

"It's just like softball, really," he said. "Keep the ball in front of you, don't try to do something you know you can't do, and never forget the fundamentals. I know I can't hit it over two hundred ten or fifteen yards now, so I don't focus on hitting it a long way. I keep it in play, stay out of trouble, and chip and putt like crazy."

Those words were barely out of his mouth when he pull-hooked a tee shot into a testy lie in a bunker on a par five. He tried to advance the next shot with a utility club and failed to get it out of the bunker. Then he topped it into the high rough. When the bloodletting was over, Leo took a nine on the hole and pitched a mild conniption fit.

"Damn it! Now I've got to par out to shoot my age. Damn it! If you can't shoot your age, there's no reason to be out here."

"That got us all square on the back," I added.

"I get shots on sixteen and eighteen."

The temper tantrum spilled over onto the sixteenth, where he missed the green to the right, chipped over the green, and failed to get up and down. That double-bogey put me one up with two to play. I shouldn't have cared, but, hey, if you can't beat an eighty-eight-year-old, there was no reason to be out here.

The seventeenth was a par three where I should have had an advantage. Leo didn't get a shot, and he was still fuming about blowing his chance at shooting his age. I figured if I could get him angry enough he might fall into one of those blabbering nursing home spasms with spittle and tremors. Then I figured I would have him for sure.

When I recounted this story later, Debbie looked at me as if I'd just confessed to being a Nazi. "You gamed an old man?" she said.

"No more than he was gaming me."

"He's almost ninety."

"Eighty-eight: He's only eighty-eight."

"I hope you live long enough for someone to treat you that way. And I hope I live long enough to see it, so I can remind you of this."

"What's to remind?" I said. "He won."

I pushed my tee shot on the par-three seventeenth into a hazard I didn't know was there. Of course, Leo knew, but had failed to tell me of the perils that awaited me if the shot leaked a little right. An octogenarian moment, I guess. He parred the hole and squared the match with one to play.

Ten minutes later he hit a perfect utility club into the center of the eighteenth green, giving himself a twelve-foot putt for birdie, net eagle, and the win. I hit my approach shot twenty feet long and missed the birdie. With the cold efficiency of a guy who once struck out twenty-five batters in a softball game, Leo rolled his first putt to within tap-in range. Before I conceded, he knocked the par putt to beat me out of ten dollars.

"Told you we'd have a great time," he said as we shook hands and I handed him a ten-dollar bill.

Part Four

Heroes

(or Don't Thank Me, I'm Just a Golfer)

SIXTEEN

The World's Toughest

Get On

(or The Green Fees Ain't Much, but the Four-Year

Commitment Is Hell)

Having already played Augusta National, Pine Valley, Butler National, Cypress Point, Seminole, Winged Foot, Muirfield, and most of the other clubs that pride themselves on their "We can play here and you can't" exclusivity, I needed a diversion, an off-the-beaten path, obscure, rough-hewn, hardscrabble, scratch-its-nails-down-your-back golf course, a hard-to-find course with only one redeeming quality: It had to be hard to get on.

I brought this up in a conversation with a friend of mine named Wendi Carpenter, a delightful mother of two who, in the history of the U.S. Navy, also happens to be the first female naval aviator to make admiral.

"There aren't many more interesting ones than the nine-hole course at Gitmo," she said.

"Gitmo?"

"Guantánamo Bay."

"Cuba?"

"The only U.S. Naval base on communist soil," she said.

"They have a golf course?"

"A nine-holer. It's not great, but it's unique."

That ranked among the great understatements of the decade. "How do you get to Gitmo?" I asked.

"You don't unless you're invited or ordered there."

"So, it might be the toughest nine-hole golf course in the world to get on," I said.

"The greens fees are cheap, but there is a four-year commitment. I'm not sure you'd make it through basic."

"Can you think of any excuse to get me down there . . . other than the four-year commitment thing?"

"Our military does great things down there," Wendi said, slipping into Rear Admiral mode without realizing it. "I'll contact the commanding officer. If you can go in your capacity as a responsible journalist . . ."

We both paused, knowing this was asking a lot.

"You'll have to be on your best behavior. No screwups if you're my guest."

"Me, screw up?" I gave her my sweetest smile.

"You can pull that on other people, but not me. Promise me you'll behave, and I'll see if I can set it up."

A few months later, Admiral Carpenter and I boarded a C-12

(the Navy version of a King Air) in Jacksonville and flew to Guantánamo Bay, where I planned to visit our troops, soak up the sun, sights, and sounds, be a "responsible journalist," and play the most difficult nine-hole golf course in the world to get on. I also planned to accompany Admiral Carpenter to the change of command. Captain Larry Cotton was going back home to Florida; Captain Mark Leary was coming to Cuba for a while. And Rear Admiral Carpenter was presiding over the ceremony.

"Watch yourself," she warned me again for the umpteenth time as we boarded the plane. "No Castro comments. These people have important jobs. They're not down here on vacation."

"Cigars?"

"Do you want me to kick you off now?"

I gave her my word that I would be good.

Once on the island, my driver, the base public affairs officer, and my tour guide, a marine corporal with one whopper of a handgun strapped to his thigh (quite an escort for someone who writes about how many fairways Tiger Woods hits), decided I needed to see the Northeast Gate, the only passageway connecting Guantánamo to the rest of the communist-controlled island. "They call Gitmo the 'Death Valley' of Cuba, because there's no fresh water and very little rain," the public affairs officer said. "Christopher Columbus discovered the place in 1494. He landed right over there." She pointed to a section of the bay near a softball and soccer complex. "He didn't stay long. He was looking for fresh water and slaves, and when he didn't find either on this end of the island he set sail for Jamaica."

"Some explorer, huh," I said.

That comment went unanswered, and we rode in silence for a minute or so until I saw the remnants of an enclosed area I recognized. The small huts, the single gate: "Hey, that looks like Camp X-Ray," I said, my mind flashing back to the not-so-distant images of detainees in orange jumpsuits, surrounded by barbed wire, on their knees outside the makeshift lean-tos.

"It is, sir," my marine escort said.

I said: "It looks abandoned." Waist-high weeds and scrap metal covered the compound, causing a serious mental disconnect. I had seen photos of this very spot as recently as a month before, complete with armed guards and shackled detainees kneeling on freshly mown grass. Now, it looked like a junkyard.

"Yes, sir," the marine told me. "Nobody has been there for three years, sir."

"Three years? You mean that footage I keep seeing on the news is three years old?"

"Yes, sir. Not only is it three years old, sir, the detainees were only there for a couple of months while we built Camp Delta. It was always temporary."

"I saw footage last month. It's three years old?"

"Yes, sir," the marine said. "Not only that, sir, CNN shot their footage from that tower"—he pointed to a watchtower on a distant hillside—"inside Cuba. I guess Castro gave them permission."

"Don't they have footage of the new camp?"

"Oh, yes, sir. They're here every week. They have plenty of recent shots. They just choose to show the footage of Camp X-Ray."

"I guess they think we can't handle the truth," I said, parroting Jack Nicholson's line from *A Few Good Men*.

"That's a good one, sir," he said, not meaning it.

The truth about Gitmo is a lot more complicated than one or two images. For all the controversy, real and imagined, spawned from our Caribbean base and the 500 Taliban and al Qaeda detainees we house there, Guantánamo Bay is not a torture chamber, or a gulag; it's not an empirical symbol, or a political football; it's not a nightstick with which to beat political opponents about the head and shoulders; and it's not a talking point for ideological zebras of either stripe. It is a forty-square-mile, 9,000-resident town where military personnel and civilians live, work, recreate, and do their duties. It has a downtown; it has subdivisions, parks, shops, theaters, an elementary and high school, a McDonald's, and a Starbucks; there's the aforementioned golf course, rental cabins on a beach near the airport, a Tiki bar (quite popular on Thursday nights when Mongolian barbecue is served), and a colonial cottage on an elevated peninsula called Deer Pointe that would fetch seven figures if it were located anywhere from Chesapeake to Montauk; there's a historical lighthouse, complete with memorabilia and a "living history" of Guantánamo Bay, as well as windmills on a distant hill (25 percent of the electricity on base is wind-generated), a reverse osmosis plant to make fresh water, a firehouse, a chapel, a phone company, numerous mini-marts, and a cable television office; it is geographically larger than Hilton Head, and has ten times more residents than Victor, Idaho.

You get a sense of Gitmo's size as you travel from one end of the base to the other at a maximum speed of twenty-five miles per hour. This sense becomes particularly acute when you're late for a tee time.

"It's that long pedal near your right foot," I said to the public affairs officer. The base Master Chief, a delightful fellow named Larry Cairo, was waiting for me on the first tee, and after flying four hours in a prop plane for this one moment, I didn't want to miss my game.

"I know, this twenty-five-mile-an-hour speed limit can be a real pain sometimes," she said.

"Ever thought of breaking it?" I asked.

"Oh, no."

"What happens if you do?"

I figured the answer would be "court martial," or "a few days in the brig."

"You get a ticket," she said.

"Big fine?"

"No bigger than back home."

"So, why don't you risk it?" I asked.

"Because it's against the law," she said, as if it were the most obvious answer in the world.

Rule breaking is a foreign concept on Guantánamo, not because of the punishment that accompanies the crime, but because it is simply not done. The streets are clean, the water is blue, the beaches are white, and the people are hellishly polite, which would make Gitmo the perfect spot for a Frank Capra film were it not for that niggling little problem of the heavily guarded fence segregating Gitmo from communist Cuba. In case you forget about the lack of friendly relations between Castro and the good people who live and work at Guantánamo Bay (as I did when I waved to one of Castro's guard towers—"no hand gestures, sir," the marine told me), the occasional explosion and smoke plume snap you back to reality. All the land mines on our side of the fence have been removed. Castro's have not. Other than that, it's a wonderful place. Even the kids are well mannered. When Captain Cotton first assumed command of the base, he asked the school principal what he needed.

"I don't really need anything," the principal said.

"Well, don't you have any problems?" the captain asked.

"Not really," he said. "We had three incidents last year, two shoving matches that didn't amount to much, and one incident where a boy and girl got a little too intimate in a broom closet, but that's it."

"All year?" Captain Cotton asked. "You have more than a thousand students, and those are the only incidents you had in an entire year?"

Coming from Jacksonville, Larry made the mistake of applying mainland values to Gitmo, a mistake every visitor makes once or twice, as I did during my initial round of golf.

Master Chief Cairo, who not only commands the enlisted personnel on the base, but is also an avid golfer and the president of the Yatera Seca Golf Association, threw my clubs on the back of a cart moments after we pulled into the gravel parking lot beside the tin-roofed cart barn. "I hope you like our golf course," he said.

"Where's the clubhouse?"

"Oh, we don't have a clubhouse. We're hoping to build a small snack area up on this hill"—he pointed as we bounced through the gravel, a cloud of dust swirling skyward in our wake. "The greens fees are free, so everybody just comes out and starts."

Then he handed me a strip of Astroturf.

"What's this for?" I asked.

He laughed and said, "Oh, you'll see. We produce all our own water on the base, two million gallons a day, so we don't have irrigation. It's too expensive. You're lucky. We average a third of an inch of rain a month. This month we've had three inches."

I sure felt lucky, and I was positive I was not going to improve my lie with artificial turf. That would defy the spirit of the game, and my entire reason for coming. By the third hole I was lifting, cleaning, and placing my strip of green Monsanto-patented synthetic turf beneath my ball.

"It's better to use the turf every time," Larry told me. "Otherwise, you never get a feel for how the ball's going to come off the hardpan."

"You know, they have some new hybrid Bermuda grasses that you can irrigate with salt water," I offered.

He smiled and shook his head. "We'd have to run the lines, and put in pump stations. There's no money for that. The Navy doesn't recognize this as a golf course. It's a 'recreational area,' which can't produce any revenue, and it has a minimal maintenance budget. That's why we have our golf association. We all pitch in and try to make it better on our own."

Larry proceeded to share his ideas for making it a better golf course. "I want to move this tee back onto that hillside. It'll add thirty yards and force you to hit it between those trees." A few holes later, he said, "You can tell there used to be bunkers in front of that green. I'd like to put them back and add crushed coral, which we have a lot of around here." Later, "You know, if we move this tee forty yards to the right, we can give the hole more definition and force you to position the tee shot—"

That's when I had to interrupt him. "These are all great ideas, Larry," I said, "but, dude, you're hitting off Astroturf."

"Good point," he said.

The second day, I partnered with the base XO, Commander Jeff Hayhurst, a great guy who was far too busy to be out playing a round of golf with the likes of me. Jeff is what the Navy calls a "Mustang," an enlisted seaman who worked his way up through the ranks and became an officer. Now he's second in command on the most famous naval base the U.S. has today. During our round, I learned that Jeff is one of thirteen children from a coal-mining family in central West Virginia. He joined the Navy to avoid spending thirty years digging coal out of the ground. He made chief in eight years, a phenomenal rise, or so Wendi informed me. Not long after my visit he made captain, which put him in the top tier of all Naval officers. As I later told Captain Larry Cotton, "If I were to have to go to war, I would want it to be with Jeff Hayhurst." Then I thought about it for a second, and added, "But if we ever reach a point where *I* have to go to war, we're screwed."

On the second hole, a 118-yard uphill par three, I saw someone step onto the green ahead of us. I elbowed Jeff, who was working overtime on his cell phone trying to coordinate the transfer of a Cuban refugee who had made it through the gate.

I pointed to the man on the green and said, "I hate to interrupt, Jeff, considering it's a guy's freedom and all, but what's going on up there?"

"Oh, he's clipping the green," Jeff said.

"Clipping the green?"

"They don't mow. We don't get enough rain for it to matter. So when the grass gets a little too long around the hole, somebody comes out and clips it."

Sure enough, the fellow clipping the second green that day was doing so with scissors.

"You missed a spot," I said.

"Very funny, sir," the man said and moved on without further comment.

As we waited for him to clear the green, I looked at an odd-shaped twelve-foot tree guarding the right side of the green. "Jeff, what kind of tree is this?" I asked.

He shook his head. "It's not a tree; it's a cactus. One of the oldest on record as near as we can tell."

I looked at the thick bark, a craggy, gnarly mesh that almost made it look like a palmetto.

"It's more than six hundred years old," Jeff said. "Columbus made note of its size in his writings, so it's survived a lot."

"Including a few incoming golf balls, I guess."

"I've certainly hit it a few times."

We both parred the second, a great uphill short hole, and we did pretty well on the third. Despite the iguanas, brick-hard fairways, and greens that had to be mowed with scissors, Yatera Seca Golf Course was not a half bad layout. The par-five fourth was a

530-yard monster playing into the teeth of the prevailing trade winds. After two blistering shots, I had to hit a six-iron from 130 yards just to get to the front of the green. Then the fifth was a great downhill 180-yard par three. And the sixth was a 430-yard par four that turned downwind, but with a tiny, elevated green, it was one of the hardest approach shots on the course.

"You could really do a lot with this place," I said to Jeff. "Bring in an architect to rework some of your features, and see if you can't get the Navy to spring for some salt-tolerant grass and irrigation, and this could be a great little golf course."

Jeff smiled and pointed to the green square at my feet. "Yeah, but right now we're hitting off Astroturf."

"Good point," I said.

After Jeff and I beat the Master Chief and his partner out of a couple of Coors Lights, my marine escort picked me up at the cart barn and drove me out to the far end of the island for a tour of Camp Delta, or as they say at Gitmo, "behind the wire."

That was when I realized we weren't in Kansas anymore. The detention facility, where uniformed men and women keep an eye on 500 battlefield combatants who didn't quite make their rendezvous with the seventy-two virgins, sits on the northern edge of the base, miles away from "downtown" Gitmo. The camp is surrounded on three sides by arid rocks and on the fourth by the Caribbean, a great piece of land if it weren't for all the barbed wire.

A mile from the compound, at our first checkpoint, soldiers carrying M-16s and 9mm sidearms opened the doors to our van and checked every ID. I was seated next to a flag officer (Admiral Carpenter) and we had the Joint Task Force information officer, an Army captain, sitting in the backseat. But we were searched thoroughly, anyway. Then the guard said, "Captain, do you vouch for everyone on board?"

A quick "Roger that," and we were on our way.

General Hood, the JTF commanding officer at the time, met us at the door of the headquarters.

"We must have caught you on the way out," I said.

He shook his head. "I knew you were coming six miles ago," he said.

Of course he did; there was no sneaking up on Camp Delta.

"How was your golf?" he asked.

"The XO and I smoked them," I said. "Sorry you couldn't join us."

The general got a big kick out of that. He and other officers laughed at my expense long after I was gone, which was fine. Their jobs were a lot more important than mine, and we all knew it.

Once we were back in the van and on our way "behind the wire" we were subjected to two more searches, one outside the first gate of the camp, and one between the first and second gates. The entrances and exits are set up like channel locks. One gate must be secured before the other is opened, with searches at every point.

Once inside, I realized that anybody who claimed we mistreat our detainees should be made to spend a few nights at the North Miami Motel 6. Sure, it was a prison—in fact one section is a brick-for-brick replica of a maximum-security penitentiary in Indiana—

but it also had a state-of-the-art hospital where wounded detainees are nursed back to health and treated for diseases so arcane that they don't have names: the crud, the rot, the black, and the red, among others. There were cells, but the structures are no worse than those at Camp America, the nearby facility that housed our own JTF forces.

"There's a review system to see where each detainee is housed," our information officer told us. "Camps one and two house those detainees who follow camp rules. They are given more privileges and get to wear white jumpsuits. That's a good color for Muslims. Camps three and four house those who don't follow all the rules, but who aren't the worst. They wear tan jumpsuits. Camps five and six house our worst offenders, and the senior al Qaeda leadership we've captured. We isolate them and force them to wear orange jumpsuits. That's an offensive color to Muslims, so we give them an incentive to behave."

"What sort of camp rules are we talking about?" I asked.

"Just following orders, not throwing urine or feces, not biting anyone, and being cooperative when we try to transport them. Pretty simple stuff."

"Throwing urine."

"Yes, sir, especially at the female troops. They don't appreciate being guarded by women. One female reservist was walking the wire [lingo for patrolling the cell blocks] and every one of the detainees threw bags of urine on her. She walked all the way down and all the way back, getting doused by every one of them. When she finished, she showered, changed her uniform, and went back and walked it again, just to show them that they couldn't get to her."

"This happened recently?"

"Oh, yes, sir. It happens a lot. That's why they're still wearing orange in those camps."

About that time, an open-bed all-terrain vehicle drove by with a white-jumpsuit detainee shackled in the back. He had a guard on either side, a driver, and a third guard in the passenger seat. As the only civilian on the premises wearing a golf shirt and seersucker slacks, I caught the detainee's attention right away. We made eye contact for no more than two or three seconds. Just long enough for every drop of blood in my body to run cold.

"So that guy is one of the trustees?" I asked.

"Oh, no, sir. The white just means he obeys camp rules."

"So, if he could get his hands on a butter knife, he'd do his dead level best to cut my head off?"

It was a rhetorical question. I didn't expect an officer of the United States Army to answer. What he did say was, "We have, through various review processes, released twenty detainees back to their home countries. Of those twenty, we have either killed or recaptured twelve on the battlefield."

"So rehabilitation isn't taking."

"That's not why we're here, sir."

Part of why they were there was intelligence. Interrogations at Gitmo had gotten a lot of scrutiny, but since I was on site as a "responsible journalist," I asked about the reasons for questioning guys who had been behind bars for five years.

"We still get actionable intelligence from these guys," the officer said. "A lot of it stems from our success in the field. The more upper-level al Qaeda guys we kill, the more likely it is that low-level grunts are promoted into leadership positions. Those low-level grunts fought and trained with a lot of the guys who are now wearing tan and white jumpsuits. That's why it's important that we keep talking to them."

Another reason I decided that the detainees didn't need to go anywhere was the tape. Every JTF soldier, sailor, airman, and marine inside the wire at Gitmo wore a strip of electrician's tape over his nametag. "What's the tape for?" I asked.

"Security," the information officer said. "When the detainees learn our names, they slip them out through their habeas corpus lawyers. That puts our families in danger."

"You have got to be kidding me."

"Oh, no, sir. In fact, there are a couple of our buddies now." He pointed to a couple of civilians waiting outside one of the administrative buildings. One of them wore a Hawaiian shirt and Mets cap.

"Your favorites, huh?" I asked.

"They're in a race with CNN for that spot," he said.

In a race for the top spot on my most-admired list were the kids I saw standing guard inside the wire at Camp Delta. I noticed it the moment we entered the gates. Every time our officer walked past an enlisted man or woman, the salutes were accompanied by a verbal exchange. The saluting soldier would say, "Honor bound, sir," and the officer would answer, "Honor bound." I had seen the slogan when we first arrived. It was on the coins, and the pamphlets; it was even painted on the ceiling above the pool tables at Rick's, the officers' bar. It surrounded a pentagon seal with a blue star and a red depiction of Cuba at its center. The caption read:

"JTF GTMO, Guantánamo Bay, Cuba: Honor Bound to Defend Freedom."

I hadn't paid much attention. Being a jaded civilian, I figured this was military sloganeering. But inside the wire, I realized it was much more than that. It was the mission these people lived for, their reason for getting up every morning and enduring what they endured. It was the reason the female reservist never missed a step as she walked the wire while urine was hoisted on her. It was the reason they put tape over their names, and said nothing while the Muslim call to prayer blared over the loudspeakers five times a day. It was the reason they never complained about eating three-dollar meals while the detainees' meals cost twelve dollars (not counting the ice cream and satellite-fed soccer matches they are treated to on Fridays).

I saw the ritual repeated no fewer than fifty times. "Honor bound, sir." "Honor bound." And I felt at once proud of my country, and ashamed of what some have said about the troops at Guantánamo Bay.

As we prepared to leave Camp Delta, Admiral Carpenter walked ahead of us, and saluted everyone who passed. When a female naval reservist snapped to attention and saluted, the admiral stopped, shook her hand, and asked the girl's name and age. She was twenty, and had been in Cuba a grand total of two weeks.

"I just want you to know how much the people back home appreciate what you're doing here," Admiral Carpenter told her. "You're making a difference. Don't ever forget that. And you need to make a mental note of everything you do here, because this might be the most important thing you ever do in your life."

The girl's lower lip began to tremble, and the dark sunglasses couldn't hide the wellspring of emotions. She saluted again, and in a cracking high voice said, "Honor bound, ma'am."

I don't know how Wendi did it, but she answered back, "Honor bound."

SEVENTEEN

Golfing Warriors

(or Playing Golf with the Greatest Generation)

If you ever hear me complain about anything in my life again, feel free to kick me in the teeth."

Those were the words of Jim Goergen, the director of instruction at Canongate Golf, a conglomeration of twenty golf courses in the Southeast. Jim is the teaching honcho for all of them. He knows his stuff, and is one of those rare golf instructors whom students will get on a plane to go see. But Jim is also popular because, in addition to knowing the ins and outs of the golf swing, he's one of those guys who never met a stranger. Everybody likes Jim.

But this day Jim was dumbfounded, stunned into a kind of wide-eyed openmouthed "holy smokes" speechlessness. At the time I was out of earshot, but I understood what was happening. Thirty yards away, on the opposite end of the flat, soggy range at Camp Lejeune, a mile from the North Carolina coast, I was hearing the same things and having the same reaction.

My charge for the afternoon was Ken Barnes, a thirty-six-year-old athlete with fast hands and the kinds of biceps you see in body-building magazines and Balco ads. As I was giving him a tip on his setup, Ken said, "My problem is grip pressure in my left hand. Shrapnel destroyed my radial artery, so I don't have much feeling. I've got to figure out how to compensate without getting too much right hand into my swing."

Before I could offer swing advice, I had to ask, "What happened?"

Gunnery Sergeant Barnes said, "We were in a convoy in Baghdad. I was walking behind a Humvee when a thousand-pound rocket exploded about fifteen feet in front of me. Thank God I had my chin strap secured. I normally kept it loose, because the helmet didn't fit right. But we got these new jell bladders that fit inside and made them real comfortable. Good thing. The blast went off and knocked me back about ten feet against the Humvee, and this huge piece of shrapnel stuck in my helmet like a big hatchet.

"The bladder burst, and I had goo running down into my eyes. When I could see, I checked my chest. Body armor was done, but I was okay. Then I checked my right arm. It was hurting, but fine. When I looked at my left arm, I said, 'Oops, not fine there.' Blood was spurting out about eighteen inches, so I stuck my right thumb into the hole and plugged what was left of the artery."

"What'd you do then?" It was a stupid question, but I could think of nothing intelligent to say, so I said anything to keep Ken talking.

"I was looking for my weapon," he said. "I wanted to go after whoever hit us. But my buddy said, 'We're okay, Gunny; you need to lie down.' They ended up removing that artery."

"Removing it?"

"Not right then, but later in the field hospital, yeah."

I was shaking my head. "I thought you needed that artery. Don't people commit suicide by cutting the thing?"

"It's better if you have it. I've regained some feeling in my hand, but you know that feeling you get when you've slept on your arm all night? I have that all the time. No big deal. The only problem now is I can't close my thumb, and my hand's cold all the time. I don't get much circulation, so I have to keep my hand in my pocket, which earns me a lot of ass-chewings from officers who don't know me."

"You get grief for this?"

"From people who don't know, yeah. I'll be in the PX, and some old officer will say, 'Your hand cold, Gunny?' I'll pull it out, show him the scars, and say, 'Yes, sir, as a strict matter of fact, it is.'"

His laugh was big and infectious. I felt compelled to join in even though I was thinking, "I can't believe I'm chuckling at a guy who almost got his arm blown off." But it was hard not to follow the lead of a guy wearing a sweatshirt that said "Pain leaves; Blood clots; Bones heal; Chicks dig scars."

When I glanced down the range, I saw that Jim wasn't engaged in any knee-slapping. He looked in shock. After I helped Gunny Barnes strengthen his left-hand grip so he could make a decent swing with a half-dead hunk of cold meat below his wrist, I excused myself and walked down to where Jim had his hands on his knees like a college coach on the sidelines of a big game.

"Have you ever been involved in anything like this in golf?" I asked.

Jim's head snapped up. He said, "I've never been involved in anything like this, ever. This might be the most life-changing thing I've ever done. Thanks for inviting me. I don't think I'll ever be the same."

None of us would, but I had no idea what kind of emotional roller coaster we were in for when I came up with the idea of playing golf with the Wounded Warriors at Camp Lejeune.

This idea didn't come to me in a dream. Like most golf freaks I keep The Golf Channel humming on the television as background noise. During one of the slower moments, I glanced up and saw Rich Lerner waxing on about a charity tournament he had attended at Camp Lejeune. There on the television I saw the fresh-faced kid with one arm hitting shots with a driver. I heard the kid talking about how he didn't want to be pitied, or viewed as disabled. He wanted to be known as a man who had served his country and would continue to live his life as a normal, productive member of society.

When the screen flipped back to Lerner, he could barely speak. He told the studio host that this was the most moving experience he had ever had as a reporter.

Wow. I knew Rich Lerner well enough to know he was not prone to hyperbole. He was a little hyper at times, and tended to take golf news (an oxymoron of the highest order) a little too seriously, but he was a pro. I had never seen him get this emotional about one of his stories, and we had covered some pretty emotional events together. I sat next to Dickey, as we call him, in the press room at the 1999 Ryder Cup when Ben Crenshaw's team came roaring back on Sunday to win. And I'd been with him a few weeks later when we covered the death of Payne Stewart. The highs and lows of golf didn't get much higher and lower than that. But I never saw Dickey lose his composure the way he lost it at Lejeune.

When I saw him again during the U.S. Open I asked him about the story, and tears welled up in his eyes. "That experience changed me," he said. "I'll never forget those guys. They were the most incredible people I've ever met."

So I did a little research, and discovered that since 2001, more than 20,000 soldiers, sailors, airmen, and marines had been injured in Iraq and Afghanistan. In previous wars, most of them would have died. Now, body armor, first aid, and field hospitals saved them. But their lives would never be the same. Walter Reed Hospital in Washington was full for the first five years of the war. Other injured servicemen were treated in San Diego. All were routed back to the real world.

Enter the Wounded Warrior Project, a relatively new nonprofit group set up to support wounded veterans, and Disabled Sports USA, another nonprofit that gets wounded veterans out of the hospital and into sporting activities. Starting at the bedside, volunteers get warriors back into society through sports. They put amputees on ski slopes in the winter, get them sailing on the Chesapeake in the summer, water skiing in New York, playing basketball on many of the bases . . . and playing golf at Camp Lejeune.

After a few phone calls I learned that Lejeune had just opened a Wounded Warrior barracks near the base golf course. Injured marines could live together and remain active in a unit while they convalesced.

"Would you guys be interested in having me over to play?" I asked. Nothing like inviting yourself to a military installation. "I might even get some instructors to come with me, put on a clinic for some of the guys."

Rule number one of being a golf freek: You never know until you ask.

"We would love to have you," Colonel Tim Maxwell said. "I'll see that it gets set up."

A month later, Jim Goergen, Tyler Dimmig (another pro who worked with Jim), and I were on the range at Camp Lejeune doing what we could to teach guys between the ages of nineteen and thirty-six how to adapt their golf swings to accommodate their injuries. One of the teenagers, a lance corporal, had a fused right knee. His biggest concern was not being able to shift his weight on the downswing. Another had taken so much shrapnel in his shoulders that he couldn't lift his arms above his head. He just wanted to generate some clubhead speed with limited motion. A third was just out of his third brain surgery since having a chunk of skull blown away. He had balance problems and wanted to stabilize his setup.

They were as upbeat and positive as any group I'd ever seen.

"I can't thank you enough for coming," Sergeant Jon Brown said as I showed him how to keep the club square during his takeaway without using the supinator, radialis, and palmarius longus muscles of his left forearm, which had been blown to smithereens.

"Jeez, please don't thank me," I said. "I should thank you guys for letting me spend time with you."

"Yeah, but you brought stuff," Sergeant Brown said with a smile.

Okay, he had me there. After Colonel Maxwell invited me to play (or that's how I advertised it), I called my tour friends from Titleist—Joe Gomes, Ann Cain, and Sandi Kelley—and said, "Look, guys, I'd love to show up at Lejeune bearing gifts. If you've got any balls or caps or anything you'd like to donate, I'll deliver them." The next week, a dozen Titleist drivers (retail value: $400 apiece), twelve dozen balls, and forty-eight caps showed up on my doorstep.

"So have you rigged this, or are all the wounded guys this up-beat?" I asked Sergeant Brown.

"We don't let them get down," he said. "That's one advantage of having everybody in a single barracks. Before, when an injured marine got out of the hospital, they said, 'Go home.' So a guy who's been injured gets separated from his unit, separated from what's going on with his buddies, and pretty much isolated. When he can't sleep, he doesn't know if it's normal, abnormal, or if he's going nuts. It doesn't take long for depression and other problems to come calling. Now we keep everybody together in a new unit. Every wounded marine has a support system. When he wakes up at two in the morning, he'll see a dozen guys walking the halls. They'll go to the rec room, play video games, and talk about it."

I was hesitant to talk. How exactly do you say, "So, corporal, how'd you get half your head blown off?" I figured that most of them were still in the "I don't want to talk about it" stage, so with the exception of my conversation with Gunny Barnes about losing his radial artery, I steered clear of asking questions.

But marines are not bashful. When a twenty-year-old lance corporal named Burroughs heard Ken telling me about the rocket going off fifteen feet away, he said, "That wasn't close, Gunny. IED that got me was a foot away." Another said, "Our truck got blown up." And another: "I got hit by a sniper."

All the stories involved something going *boom* and bad things happening as a result. Suddenly, the war seemed a lot more real.

Jim shook his head at me and said, "Man, this is unbelievable."

A couple of minutes later we stood motionless, chills running down our backs, as one of the sergeants shared his story in a quiet monotone voice. "We were moving from one hot spot to another when our truck ran over an IED. It blew all of us out. I flew about thirty feet, landed on my back with a bunch of junk in me, so I couldn't move. My best friend was blown sixty feet away into a canal. I was lying there, yelling, not able to move . . ." he paused and twitched. "I watched my best friend drown. Nobody could get to him."

After a few seconds of silence, Jim said to the kid, "What are your plans now?"

"Get better and go back," he said.

"Go back?"

"Yes, sir. Guys from my unit are still over there. I'm going back."

That was a standard theme. All of the warriors wanted to go back.

"The commandant of the Marine Corp says if these guys want to stay in, they can stay in," Gunny Barnes told us. "The Marines will find a job for them. Some choose to get out, some choose to move into noncombat units, but most of the guys here want to go back and join their units."

"Are they actually going back?" I asked. "It's one thing to want to, but—"

"Most are, yeah," Ken said. "We had this one kid, Sanchez, who had his entire forehead blown off. Pretty amazing, but he didn't have any brain damage. The bone around the wound had to calcify before they could put a permanent plate in his head. So, the doctors gave him this temporary plastic thing to cover the wound. He tied it onto his head with a bandana. Talk about somebody giving people the jitters.

"I was in the PX with him one day, and I heard this old chief warrant officer yell, 'Come here, shithead.' He started chewing on the kid for wearing a bandana with his fatigues. After about five minutes of ass-chewing I said, 'Show him, Sanchez.' He untied that rag and half his head fell out in his hand. That chief warrant officer's eyes got the size of hubcaps."

"What did he say?"

"He just grunted and said, 'Oh.'"

"Sanchez didn't go back."

"Oh, yeah," Ken said. "He got a titanium plate, which he loved because he could stick refrigerator magnets to his forehead. But he's back in Iraq now."

That's when Jim patted me on the back and said, "If you ever hear me complain about anything in my life again, feel free to kick me in the teeth."

The next day, we played the Scarlet course at Lejeune. I suggested a scramble format, since some of the guys would have had trouble chasing balls all day. Lance Corporal Burroughs could barely get out of the cart without using clubs as crutches. But that didn't stop him from hitting every tee shot and doing his best on every putt.

"Putting shouldn't be a problem," he said. "I can set up on my left side and make a decent stroke."

Lance Corporal Sardinas couldn't feel his right arm or close his right hand, which made it tough to hit a tee shot. "But, hey, it's better than losing an arm," he said. "I can still lend you a hand."

"Funny, Sardinas," Ken said.

"No other way, Gunny."

"Are you thinking about going back?" I asked Ken.

"I can't," he said. "I can't reload my weapon or pull myself up with my left arm. I gave it a good shot, but there's no way. Thankfully, I've got the Wounded Warrior Barracks. That's my unit now."

"You think that'll be a permanent gig for you?"

He nodded and looked at the wind blowing the flag on the second green. "If you're a specialist, corporal, or sergeant in Iraq, you've got a one in twelve chance of being wounded, and a one in twenty-four chance of being killed. As long as we're at war, there'll be a need for what we're doing."

I didn't speak for the next three holes. That changed when Sergeant Brown beaned a blind man in the forehead.

Lance Corporal Tussi had taken shrapnel to the temple, which would have killed him twenty years ago. Now he was just 80 percent blind. Given time to focus, he could see still objects, but he had no depth perception and couldn't see a thing once it moved. He also had been a pretty good golfer, a skill he hoped to retain despite his injury. "If I take my time setting up, I can see the ball," he said. "I just can't follow it after I hit it."

Nor could he see it when it was thrown at him, which was what Sergeant Brown did on the seventh hole. Tucci hit a great putt, which Brown conceded. The sergeant then picked up the ball and tossed it to a blind man. To his credit, Tucci attempted to make a grab. He only missed by four feet. When the ball bonked Tucci in the head, everyone in the group, including Tucci, doubled over in laughter.

When we finished the round, Colonel Maxwell and Gunnery Sergeant Barnes thanked us again for coming.

"God, I wish you wouldn't do that," I said.

"Hey, we want you to come back," Ken said.

"Next time I'll bring more instructors and equipment. We'll make it a big deal."

"Or come by yourself," Ken said. "You're always welcome. We're not going anywhere."

It was sad, but I left knowing Ken's last statement was a cold, hard fact. As long as there were wounded marines, they weren't going anywhere. And it looked like that need was going to be around for a long, long time.

EIGHTEEN

Son of a Freekin' Golfer

(or How Your Progeny Makes You Proud)

The hardest lesson I learned from my first marriage is that no matter how good the intentions or how civil the separation, children suffer when parents divorce. One parent, usually the father, becomes a visitor. Many a man has tried to stave it off, but the sad truth of a broken marriage is that when your children live under another roof you slowly slip into an oh-by-the-way afterthought, someone who isn't there for the mundane moments of life, and who therefore can be forgotten when bigger events roll around.

I didn't intend for things to go south with my older children—most fathers don't—but life happens. You keep up with report cards until they stop arriving in the mail. You ask questions long after you stop getting answers. Frustration slides into resignation as visits get shorter and excuses grow. Weekends turn into "Dad, some friends want me to come over to their place this Saturday." Friday dinners become "I've got a game." And holidays at home morph into "Can I go to the beach with my classmates?"

Before you know it, you're attending the high school graduation of a kid you barely know.

My oldest son is James Stephen Jr., a child I loved enough to give my name. After his mother and I split up, he didn't speak to me for a year. I couldn't blame him; I was the one who packed up and moved into another house. Things didn't get much better when I married Debbie and started another family. My older children love their brother and sister, but their relationship with them is different: expected, to be sure, but another in the death of a thousand cuts most divorced fathers endure.

When James graduated from high school it had been a month since I had talked to him. What few conversations we'd had prior to that were stilted and vague.

"Have you decided where you're going to school?"

"I've got options. Things are still up in the air."

"When do you expect to make a decision?"

"Soon. I'll let you know."

"Is there anything I can do?"

"No, I'm good."

But I went to his graduation ceremony to congratulate him, get a few pictures, and let him know that even though he was almost nineteen, I was around if he needed me.

When all of those duties were complete, in the middle of a scrum of graduates, I gave the college question one more shot.

"So do you know where you're going?" I asked.

"Yeah, I do."

"May I ask where?"

"Parris Island."

"What!"

"I'm going into the Marine Corps."

"You what?" I turned to his mother and yelled, "Did you know about this?"

She put her hands up and said, "I had nothing to do with it. He did this on his own."

My legs almost failed, and I wobbled for a second.

"James you're an honor graduate, an A student. What about college?"

"I'm going," he said. "I've signed up for the Reserves, so after I go through basic, specialist training, sniper school, jump school, and some other stuff, I'll be assigned to a reserve unit. They'll put me through college after that. When I graduate, I can be an officer."

"Is that what you want to do?"

"Yeah, it is. I'll probably make it a career."

When I was nineteen, my career thoughts extended no farther than the next keg party and the girl who wore halter tops and terrycloth shorts to economics class every Friday. My son was joining the Marines at a time when a casualty a day was coming home in a flag-draped box.

"Are you sure about this?"

"I'm sure," he said. "This is what I want to do. And it's what I'm doing."

Four months later, and one week before he was to report to Parris Island, South Carolina, for thirteen weeks of pure hell, I called James and asked if he could sneak out for a quick Saturday afternoon round of golf. "We'll play with Frank at his club," I said, referring to my father. I dangled the prospect of seeing his grandfather as an enticement. I doubted he would come if it was just he and I. Plus, I wasn't sure when all three of us would be together again. James's training schedule would keep him hopping for eighteen months or more. If his reserve unit was called up, it might be years before we saw him again. Frank was sixty-seven with three heart surgeries under his belt. He was too ornery to die, but I wasn't sure how many more eighteen-hole rounds he had left in the tank.

"Yeah, that's fine," James said. "I don't have my clubs."

"Son, I have plenty of golf clubs. What make and model would you like?"

"Whatever you've got."

"You'll meet us at the course?"

"On my way."

Pebble Beach or the Plantation Course at Kapalua would have been a more romantic setting to conclude my Golf Freek odyssey. But the fact that I would call it quits at a small nine-hole course called Arrowhead Country Club, in the even smaller town of Jasper, Georgia (the southern starting point for the Appalachian Trail, and home of the world's largest Jeep dealership), didn't bother me in the least. I was playing with my father and my oldest son. We could have whacked balls around an alpaca ranch and I would have been happy.

James showed up on the first tee wearing a scarlet and gold T-shirt with the eagle, anchor, and globe symbol of the Marines on the front. He had gained fifteen pounds of muscle in four months, and I stopped walking and did a double take when I saw him. His upper arms were bigger than my legs. We had never looked alike. He was five foot eight and stocky, with a neck that fanned out to broad shoulders and thighs that strained the stitches on his jeans. His waist tapered like a funnel, which made his clothes look odd. The shirt was tight around his big chest and loose near the belt, which was drawn tight.

"How much do you weigh now?" I asked.

"Not quite two-ten."

I was three inches taller and had never tipped the two-hundred-pound mark in my life.

"Your recruiter thinks that's a good number?" Frank asked as he came out of the golf shop.

"I'll probably get bigger. You're required to eat a ton of calories."

"Yeah, but you burn a ton, too," Frank said. He knew. When I was one month old, Lieutenant Frank Eubanks left Fort Benning in the middle of the night and boarded a ship bound for Cuba, where a cranky old Russian had parked a bunch of nukes. He never saw combat, but he knew what James was in for a lot better than I did. Frank reached the rank of captain before getting out; the nearest I'd come to service was giving golf lessons to a couple of generals, and buying drinks in an airport bar for some guys in fatigues who had just come home.

"How are you coming with your PFT?" Frank asked.

"PFT?" Jeez, he hadn't reported to basic yet and the acronyms were already flying.

James and Frank said, "Physical fitness test," at the same time.

Then Frank said, "So, how's it going?"

"I ran three and a half miles this morning in twenty-five minutes."

"Sit-ups?"

"A hundred in two minutes."

"What else?"

"I did forty chin-ups."

"Forty chin-ups," I said. "That's where you pull yourself up until your chin touches a bar, right?"

"Right."

"You did forty of those?"

"I'm sure I'll get to where I can do more."

"How many of those are you up for, Dad?" I asked.

"I'm retired."

"How about you?" James said to me.

"I'm going to say . . . two."

"I'll take the under on that," Frank said as he teed up a ball and hit the opening shot of our round.

James and I rode in a cart for a little father-son bonding. Frank's club didn't allow walking on weekends, a rule so insulting to the spirit of the game that I asked Dad what the hell the members were thinking.

"They need the cart revenue."

"You didn't pay for this round, did you?"

He might have assumed my indignation was based on chivalry: that I thought I should pay for our group since this was, after all, my idea. Of course that was not the case. I wanted to make sure we were playing for free.

"No, they comped us," he said. "I told them what you were doing, and that James was on his way to Parris Island."

"They bought that?" James said.

Frank pointed his thumb at me. "Hard to believe with this one in the group," he said. "You'd think they would have wised up by now."

I hit my tee shot and said, "I've been comped at better and worse."

"Story of your life," James said. "Sliding by."

I didn't let him see how much that one hurt. He was nineteen and about to put his life on the line for things like duty, honor, and country. I was sponging free golf. A fine example I was.

"I think I'll hit five-iron," James said.

"You can hit more than that here," I said. "Take three-wood at the corner of those left trees."

"No, I like hitting five-iron. I score pretty well when that's all I hit."

"You know, I played with the four-time world one-club champion not long ago," I said. "He's in the record books for shooting the lowest round on record with one club."

James cocked his head, and said, "Your point?"

"He plays with a six-iron."

"Five is fine."

He swung like a guy who'd done forty chin-ups that morning: a violent whipping action that was accompanied by a primal grunt. The ball flew thirty yards right of target, but stayed in play.

"Think you could swing any harder?" Frank asked.

"I'm sure I can," he said. "I'm just getting warmed up."

As promised, James played every shot outside 100 yards with a five-iron, which he hit anywhere from 101 to a stout 215. The swing never got any smoother, but he straightened out the sidespin. By the eighth hole, he was hitting the center of the fairway. After he made two straight pars on eight and nine, I figured it was a good time to have the talk I'd been putting off for a couple of hours that afternoon, and for a couple of years before that.

"What exactly will your job be once you get through basic?" I asked as my lead-in.

"Recon."

"What's that?"

"It's short for reconnaissance."

"I know what Recon is. I mean, what exactly is the job?"

"It's the Marine Corps version of the Navy SEALS or the Army Special Forces. 'Course, Force Recon is a lot more elite. We'll do amphibious missions, ordnance delivery support . . ."

"Whoa, what's that?"

"It's where we go into hot zones and designate targets, like pointing out the house where the bad guys are, that sort of thing. Counterterrorism, prisoner rescue, air insertion. Jump school will be at Benning. I think sniper school's in Hawaii."

I became immediately aware that my shirt had been given to me by some club marketing director. The shoes I had on were gifts from FootJoy, and both sets of clubs James and I were using had been free.

"Can I send you anything at Parris Island?" I asked.

"No." He stepped closer and shook his head. "Don't send anything except small letters on plain white paper. No boxes, no care packages, nothing. Not only will I not get it, I'll catch endless shit for it."

"Got that Marine vocabulary working already," Frank shouted from the other side of the fairway.

We both ignored him. I had more pressing things to worry about than my son's salty language, which he'd heard from me since he was eating Gerber's.

"Do you think you'll go overseas?" I asked.

"If things don't change . . . yeah, probably."

I fumbled for what to say. Then, after James hit another low, screaming five-iron up the right side of the fairway, I said, "I want you to do a couple of things for me."

"What's that?"

"Don't make the mistakes I've seen a lot of guys make when they join. Don't get married, and don't get a tattoo—"

"I have no intention of getting a tattoo," he interrupted. "As for getting married, I've seen how that can turn out. I won't be going there for a while."

Another well-deserved zinger to the heart. I hoped he was that accurate with a sniper rifle.

I coughed to stall, but when I realized James had nothing else to say, I plunged ahead. "A couple of other things," I said.

"Uh-huh?"

"Stay alive and come home."

"That's the plan."

"No, I'm serious."

"So am I."

"And . . . just so you know . . . I know this is going to sound all sappy and fatherlike, but . . . I'm really proud of you. You've made great choices in your life, things I couldn't imagine doing when I was your age. You just need to know . . . it makes me feel great to see the things you've done."

He shrugged and said, "You're right, that was pretty sappy and fatherlike." Then after a pause where I stepped off the distance of my next shot and pulled a utility club out of my bag, James said, "It's called growing up."

He didn't say, "You should try it some time." He didn't have to.

James made another par and a slew of bogeys with his five-iron. Frank played pretty well, too, although he did so with a full complement of clubs. I remember making par on the final hole, but on the whole, the golf was so meaningless I didn't bother adding up my score.

"Thanks for asking me to come out," James said as he threw his shoes in the back of his Jeep.

"Thanks for coming," I said as I approached him awkwardly. I had given James hugs every time I'd seem him since I divorced his mother. But after he turned twelve, he became adept at dodging, turning his body to thwart any full-body contact. That hadn't stopped me from trying, a fact I was thankful for when I approached him this time.

For the first time in seven years, my son hugged me with both arms, his cheek pressed to mine. He didn't back away, and he didn't let go. Thankfully, I didn't have to say anything. We held

each other in the parking lot for about ten seconds. Then he patted me on the back, and said, "I've got to run."

"I'll see you at graduation. Thirteen weeks."

"I'll be there."

I don't remember changing shoes or putting my clubs away. I
do remember collapsing in the front seat of my father's car and
staring out the window at a guy in knee-length shorts flailing away
on the driving range.

"He'll be fine," Frank said as he cranked the car. "He's a
good kid. He knows what he wants to do, and I'm sure he'll be
good at it."

That was meant to assuage my worry, and I appreciated the effort. But that wasn't what I was feeling. Sure, I was concerned for
my son's safety. The words from Camp Lejeune rang in my head
like a cowbell: "Specialists, corporals, and sergeants in Iraq have a
one in twelve chance of being injured, and a one in twenty-four
chance of being killed." A lot could change in the eighteen
months James would be in training; still, those stats banged
around my noggin like a pinball. But I also felt something else. As
I slouched in the passenger seat of my father's car, I felt like the
things I had done—the golf I'd played, the people I'd met, the
places I'd been, and the things I'd written—didn't really amount
to much. Somehow, I had figured out a way to eke out a living
chasing a ball around a manicured garden, and then writing
about it. If someone had asked me about retirement I would have
said, "What would I retire to? All I do is play golf and write. Are
you going to make me stop?" It was a sporty way to pay the bills.
And that afternoon, it felt completely inadequate.

"He really went after that five-iron, didn't he?" Frank said with a slight chuckle.

"I can't believe he made contact swinging that hard," I said.

Golf was the sanctuary for all conversations in my family. If a subject got too squishy, just mention a tee shot from some long-ago round or the latest news from any of the tours, and you could tack the listing discussion back to safe harbor.

"I'm glad he came up today," Frank said. "It's probably the last round he'll play for a good long time."

"It was great seeing him," I said, and left it at that. I knew that if I tried to utter what was screaming through my brain, the words would never make it out of my mouth. To verbalize the realization that "Gee, in forty-four years I've never looked up to anybody as 'my hero' until today, and lo and behold, it turns out to be my son" would have been too much.

I didn't feel like bawling all over Frank's dash. So when Vince Gill came on the radio, I hummed the melody and tried to focus on the words.

"You playing any more this week?" Frank asked.

I shook my head without taking my eyes off the road. "No," I said without much conviction. "Time to pack it in."

"Think you've got enough for that free-golf book you're supposed to be writing?"

"Oh yeah," I said. "I've got plenty. Now I just need to go home, hang the clubs up for a while, and hug the kids."

Frank laughed so hard both car seats shook. "Bullshit," he said. "You'll be out hitting balls before Wednesday."

I had to smile. He was right. And we both knew it.

Lessons from a Golf Freek

(or Don't Ever Take It for Granted)

For the last years of his life, I had a close friendship with Mark McCormack, the founder of IMG, the world's largest sports management firm, and the man credited with creating sports marketing. I used to joke that Mark was my only billionaire friend, but you only need one. He was a successful self-made man, a fantastic guy who befriended me, someone who was thirty-five years his junior and who could do absolutely nothing for him. In our time together, Mark taught me a great deal about leadership, business, and how to deal with people. But he also taught me invaluable lessons about life, lessons I try to pass along to others.

One of the best lessons I learned from Mark came in New York during the U.S. Open tennis championship. He had asked me to come up to his Upper East Side brownstone for a meeting, which wasn't much of a meeting at all: more of a gab session on books, sports, entertainment, politics, and any other subject that popped into our heads. Several people from the company were there, including a fellow named Chuck Bennett, who ran IMG Models, the fashion division of Mark's empire. Chuck managed Heidi Klum and Gisele Bundchen, among others. At some point in the middle of our chat, Chuck asked, "Oh by the way, Mark, do you have a couple of extra tickets to the Open for tomorrow night?"

Mark cocked his head and said, "For whom?"

"Oscar de la Renta was asking."

Mark smiled and said, "Tell Oscar I'll work on it and get back to him."

I thought this was odd, because I knew Mark had a stack of tickets in the breast pocket of his jacket. He had pulled them out before the others arrived and asked me if I wanted to go. I had to pass; my flight home was early the next morning. But I wasn't on the same page as Oscar de la Renta. I couldn't figure out why Mark would put off a simple request like that.

Several months later, when Mark and I were playing our annual golf match at Isleworth, I asked him about the ticket incident in New York. "You could have dealt tickets around the table like playing cards," I said. "Why didn't you give Chuck those tickets for Oscar de la Renta?"

"I did, eventually," he said. "Chuck passed the message back that I was working on it. The next morning, Chuck called again and said, 'Any news on those tickets for Oscar?' I told him I was still working on it, but I would have an answer for him by noon. At noon, I called Oscar myself and told him I not only had tickets for him, but that he was getting seats just above the players' boxes."

"But why the long dance?" I asked.

"Because if I had just pulled them out of my pocket, their value wouldn't have been appreciated: It would have seemed like a small thing. I don't mean monetarily small; I mean valuable in terms of getting the hard to get, doing the hard to do. Do you understand?"

I looked out at the beautiful Isleworth course in front of us. A half hour earlier I had warmed up on the range with Charles Howell III on my left and Stuart Appleby on my right. It wouldn't be unusual if Tiger came into the clubhouse for a hamburger while we were there.

"I hope you know I appreciate this," I said.

He smiled and said "That's why you get invited back."

The moral of this story is simple: Value is never found on a price tag. True worth is measured in respect and appreciation. The free golf I have played in my life—thousands of rounds with a total retail price stretching into the high six figures—has been more valuable to me than money. And the appreciation I have for those who had me as their guest is as priceless as the lasting friendships I have made.

Golf is a game that no one will ever master. That's why we keep playing. But more compelling than the game itself are the friendships and shared experiences we discover through golf, the relationships we rekindle, and the lasting memories we create.

Those things, like the price of my golf, might be free. But their value is immeasurable. Keep them close to you forever, and you will have found the secret.

ACKNOWLEDGMENTS

Who on earth do you thank when you need to thank everybody? That is the dilemma facing anyone who plays a lot of "you are our guest today" golf. When the entire premise of the book is based on the goodwill of those who are willing to tolerate your free-loading ways, you're bound to miss somebody.

I know I could never thank everyone who helped me in small and large ways in preparing for this book. But there are some who deserve a shout-out. Among them, I owe a special thanks to Mark Reiter and Luke Dempsey, who believed in this zany idea even when I had doubts of my own; to Steve Ross at Crown for his continued friendship and support, and Sean Desmond, who did yeoman's work on a short deadline. More thanks go out to Emily Sklar, Arnold Palmer, Donald "Doc" Giffin, Cory Britt, J. S. Kang, Jeong Jang, Larry Dorman, Alice Cooper, Tony George, Clay Long, John Strege, Butch Harmon, Cindy Reid, Jack Lumpkin, Brad King, Wally Uihlein, Ann Cain, Joe Gomes, Buddy Darby, Joanne Stemple, Stephanie Branston, Terry Lazar, Admiral Wendi Carpenter, CMDC Larry Cairo, Commander Jeff Hayhurst, Gunnery Sergeant Ken Barnes, Ted Lennon, the family of Mark H. McCormack, Alastair Johnston, Thad Daber, Al Geiberger, and Dr. Phil Lee.

And to everyone who has put up with me—you know who you are—I offer heartfelt and warm thanks.